Using Number Lines

with 5–8 year olds

Fran Mosley

British Library Cataloguing-in-
Publication Data

A catalogue record for this book is
available from the British Library.

Written by
  Fran Mosley

Designed and typeset by
  Joan Roskelly

Edited by
  Jill Brand

Photographs by
  Len Cross
  Sally Greenhill

Cover by
  Emma Whiting

Illustrated by
  Bill Le Fever

Published by
  BEAM Education, Maze Workshops,
  72a Southgate Road, London N1 3JT

Printed by
  Print-source, Great Britain

ISBN 1 874099 95 2

Contents

Introduction

There are two vital, and complementary, images of number which underpin much of our mathematical understanding: numbers as labels or a collection of objects (the 'set' model); and ordered numbers, with regular, identifiable patterns such as odd and even. This latter is the 'number line' model.

Many of our strategies for mental calculation rely on a secure grasp of order and pattern in the number system – and can be very simply illustrated on a number line. And if we are confident in manipulating numbers, we can pick and choose strategies according to the specific problem. Developing this flexibility in mental mathematics is a key aim of the National Numeracy Strategy, and the physical number line is a powerful tool in achieving it. Many of the mental calculation strategies suggested in the *Framework for Teaching Mathematics from Reception to Year 6* are based on images of number lines and, later, on the empty number line. The *Framework* also stresses the value of using number lines for jottings.

This book aims to help children to develop a sound understanding of ordered numbers and then use this effectively in calculations. The activities offer children different visual representations of ordered number, from curved lines of whole numbers to fraction lines and lines showing only the multiples of five. Children progress from using fully numbered lines and tracks, to marked but unnumbered lines, finally making the key transition to the more powerful and flexible empty number line towards the end of Key Stage 1.

How this book is organised

This book is organised into three main parts. The first consists of quick starter activities to practice recognising numerals, counting and calculating with the four types of line: number tracks, numbered lines, unnumbered lines and empty lines.

The second part shows how the four types of line can be used to teach seven key mathematical topics. Most of the activities are suitable for the main part of the daily mathematics lesson; all are clearly linked to the objectives in the National Numeracy Strategy. There is no need to work through the activities in order – just choose to suit your need.

The third part consists of photocopiable resource sheets and number lines.

The four kinds of track or line

Number tracks

The first representation of a number sequence that most children will see is the number track or frieze on their bedroom wall, or in their classroom. Each number occupies a square and may have a matching illustration. These tracks support children in learning to read the numerals, and in locating ordered numbers.

The numerals on these tracks number the *squares*, in the same way that seat numbers in the cinema number the seats: the first is '1', the second is '2', and so on. So we can look at any square (or cinema seat) and know how many come before it.

This is why number tracks should start at 1, not 0: each number represents a numbered object. Counting the squares or cinema seats would become very confusing if the first was labelled '0'!

Number tracks can be linear, zigzagged (like a snakes and ladders board), or cut and layered (like a 100-grid or number cards). They can be arrayed horizontally or vertically.

Children can use number tracks to solve various problems. Young children might count their toy bears by putting one on each square starting at '1': if there is one bear on each square up to and including '5', then they know they have five bears. However, children may have difficulties when they use number tracks for counting on, such as in 'Snakes and ladders'. The question for the child is whether or not to count the square they are already on.

one two three
↓   ↓   ↓

| 1 | 2 | 3 | 4 | 5 | 6 | 7 | 8 |

"three more than 4 is 7"

Encourage children to count the *steps* forwards or backwards, rather than the squares. You can also help them move on to using number lines, where the whole focus is on making and counting steps.

Numbered lines

Numbered lines have numbers at regular intervals along the line, their positions indicated by marks. Commercially produced lines may be intended for photocopying, or printed on wipe-clean material for repeated use; you can write out your own lines on paper, on the board or even on the floor or playground.

When children first meet and use number lines, it is important that they realise it is the marks, not the spaces between, that are numbered. This is a significant difference between number lines and number tracks: on tracks the numbers belong to the spaces.

A number line encourages children to draw and count steps forwards or backwards, which avoids the 'number-track problem' of whether or not to count the starting number. Lines can show any number sequence: 0 to 50, 90 to 100, –10 to +10, … and can be numbered in ones, twos, fives, tens, … The first numbered lines that children meet will show numbers to 10, 20 or 30 and will begin at zero (rather than 1, as on a number track), indicating that at the start of the line no steps have yet been taken.

One useful aspect of number lines is that they allow the continuous nature of number to be represented. As adults we are aware that between the whole numbers are other numbers, which we describe as fractions or decimals. As children's grasp of the number system develops, they too need to develop this understanding.

Crucially, number lines encourage children of all ages to develop useful mental strategies such as:

to add 18 and 6, start at 18, add on 2 (pausing on 20) and then the remaining 4: 18 + 6 = (18 + 2) + 4 = 20 + 4 = 24.

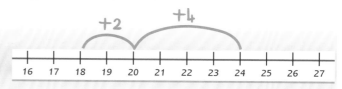

Unnumbered lines

In this book the term 'unnumbered lines' is used to mean lines with markers which are either completely free of numbers, or where only landmarks such as multiples of five are numbered. Both of these kinds are available commercially, as are counting sticks – sticks divided into sections which can be numbered as you choose.

These unnumbered lines encourage children to build on what they have learnt about the structure of number lines and of the number system. By providing markers but few, or no, actual numbers, they require children to think for themselves about where numbers belong. Structured work with completely unnumbered lines can help children grasp two key ideas about number lines: that they need not start at zero; and that the divisions may indicate steps of different sizes, not always ones.

Children can fill in unnumbered lines with sequences such as the numbers from 90 to 110, multiples of 10, fractions, … They can use number lines with only the fives and tens written in for calculations using steps and jumps of various sizes. (Lines numbered in ones may encourage the habit of counting on in ones even when larger steps would be more efficient.) These lines provide a stepping stone towards the empty number line, which in itself is a step towards purely mental calculation, using mental imagery rather than any physical line of numbers.

The empty number line

Printed or drawn number lines are suitable while children are learning the skills needed to calculate mentally and on paper. But if children work for too long with numbered or marked lines, they may continue to rely on these props long after they are appropriate. For this reason, it is important to introduce empty number lines as soon as children seem ready, particularly for recording the steps in mental calculations. Children will need to spend some time working on empty number lines alongside other lines, before they are confident enough to rely on empty lines alone. Even then they may want to revert to numbered or marked lines at times; make sure they can do so, and encourage them back to empty lines when they feel confident.

Important skills that children need to hone before they can make good use of empty number lines are:

- making jumps of different sizes, especially tens
- moving confidently both forwards and backwards on the numbered line
- using the number complements to 10 and later to 20
- breaking and recombining numbers (for example, seeing 7 + 5 as 7 + 3 + 2, or 28 + 9 as 28 + 10 − 1)

The best way of introducing empty lines is to demonstrate them as a recording method when you discuss mathematics with the class. Children will see how you use these lines and can begin to adopt them as a method of recording.

Helen worked out 34p and 79p by starting with the 79 and adding one, to take her to 80, then three tens ... 90, 100, 110, and then the last 3 ... 113 which is £1.13.

Because empty number lines are sketches they do not need to be drawn to scale, although it is often helpful to acknowledge the different sizes of numbers by making, say, jumps of ten larger than jumps of five.

Empty number lines really come into their own in problem solving when they can act as sketched records of the intermediate steps in a calculation. They are a valuable tool which children can use to support their mental work, whether dealing with addition, subtraction, multiplication or division, or a combination of these operations.

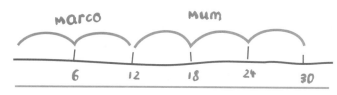

When they went shopping, Marco put two eggboxes, each with six eggs, in the trolley.

His mum put in three more boxes.

How many eggs did they have altogether?

Jumps of different sizes

When children first draw on a number line it is easiest for them to make single steps.

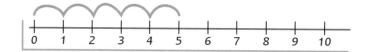

Use a demonstration line to show children how to draw equal jumps. Explain that you are going to draw jumps of two and that each jump is like two steps in one. Ask the children to help you make sure the jumps are all the right size.

Also show how to draw larger jumps, of three, four or five. Invite children to draw jumps on the demonstration number line.

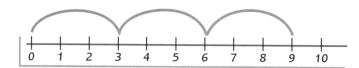

Children who need more support

Many children experience difficulties with mathematics at some time or another. While it is important to present activities simply and clearly to children struggling, it is also important not to do everything for the child or to remove all the challenge. Diagnostic questioning will help to reveal where the specific difficulty lies. It is best to do this in a small group or one to one with the child, without interruption or distraction – for either the teacher or the child. Children often develop excellent coping or concealing strategies, and careful observation of their methods and attentive listening to their explanations will be needed. Questions should be of both the open and closed variety, for example:

Can you tell me how you did that?
Can you draw the steps on the number line?

What number comes before/after ...?

If I draw this on the number line, what question could you ask that would need this for the answer?

Why do you think Nicola did that? Was she right to do that?

How would you have solved that problem?

Many problems stem from children not knowing the counting words confidently. While we spend a lot of time helping the youngest children learn to count, we sometimes stop teaching the pattern of words too soon, before the children are really confident. This is particularly true of counting in steps other than one and counting backwards.

Learning to count involves several stages. First, children must learn to say the number names in order as an unbroken chain; this is rather like learning the words to a song and needs to be automatic. At this stage children will need to begin at the beginning; learning to start the 'song' at any point, as a broken chain, comes later and it is this skill that enables children to develop a 'count on' strategy. For this, they will need to learn to count both forwards and backwards and to know which numbers come before and after a given number.

Children generally become confident to 10 fairly quickly but the 'teen' and 'ty' numbers can cause problems. Listen very carefully to children as they count and be ready to correct.

A common problem is: '... 9, 10, 11, 12, 30, 40, 50 ...'

and similarly: '10, 20, 30, 14, 15, 16, 17, 18, 19, 20.'

Point out and correct such errors, explaining what the children may have done wrong so that they understand the potential pitfalls. Ordering digit cards and filling in numbers on number lines, as well as correct naming of the written numerals, all help with these problems. Children who continue to experience difficulties with the 'teens' could work in the 20s and 30s while they sort out this bit of their counting.

Children with special circumstances, such as visual impairment or poor motor skills, can be accommodated by careful design of the number line (extra large numerals and wider spacings) and with numeral cards on thicker board.

You will find suggestions for working with children who need more support under 'Variations' in many of the activities.

Children who are more confident

The use of any number line is not an end in itself; the aim is for children to develop mental strategies based on the models provided by the line. Children who display the confidence to carry out the calculations correctly without a line should be encouraged to do so. Encourage children who are normally confident, but make errors, to explain how they carried out the mental calculation, while you act as scribe and draw the steps and jumps for them; this can often help children see where they have gone wrong, without you pointing out their error. For example:

'I added 7 to 28 by adding on 2 to get thirty and then another four to 34.'

Once again, the 'Variations' often provide suggestions for encouraging and challenging the more confident children.

Number scripts and other languages

Some children whose home or first language is not English might have come across a different number script. This can be a wonderful resource. Older children or parents – or members of staff – could help make numeral cards and number lines to show the class that numbers exist in other scripts and languages, and that mathematics transcends language and culture.

Most modern number systems use place value in base 10, and the similarities between these systems are evident in the repeating patterns which occur in the decades. With the children, compare two or more differently scripted number lines, and try to identify these patterns.

If you have the resources, you could make tapes of people counting rhythmically in different languages – whether or not the language uses a different script. Listen to these tapes while looking at the numerals on an ordinary 0–100 number line; it is often easy to follow even a language you don't speak as the decades repeat the familiar patterns of number words.

Inventing and adapting games

Children may enjoy helping you to make up games on number lines based on favourite stories, a recent outing, current events in school or the community, or more well-known games, and will have fun playing them afterwards.

If you develop a game with a specific learning outcome in mind (for example, learning to count on or sequencing events), you may find that children subvert your best intentions by creating fantasies or narratives around the game and losing interest in the mathematics. You may need to cut down the 'context' aspects of the game in order to focus the children back on the mathematics.

One way to adapt a game is to use a 'what if not' activity. First of all, think of all the conditions that prevail when you play a game, then think what would happen if each condition were changed. The following example shows the process with 'Snakes and ladders', where any one change gives you a new game.

⬤ Snakes and ladders	⬤ What if not …
board marked 1–100	• board marked 2–200, counting in twos
numbers 'snake' from bottom left to top left	• board set out on a horizontal or vertical number line with 'scaffolding' joining squares
dice 1–6	• dice marked with even numbers only • 0–9 dice
start at beginning and move forwards	• start at 50 and use dice marked +2, +4, +6 and –1, –2, –3 to move both backwards and forwards
snakes go down; all different lengths	• any point marked with a snake means go back nine places
ladders go up; all different lengths	• any point marked with a ladder means go forward eleven places
move tokens	• draw steps on number line – one player above the line, one below

Resources and equipment

Making your own number lines

Whether or not you have commercially produced number lines (see page 15), there will be times when you want to make your own, perhaps because the children need lines to write on or because you want a line numbered in a particular way. At the back of this book you will find photocopiable lines which you can copy, cut up and stick together as necessary. If appropriate, they can then be laminated or covered with clear film.

The activities in this book require tracks and lines in three sizes:

- **floor**, which are particularly useful for younger children who can experience literally taking steps forwards and backwards on them;
- **demonstration**, which should be large enough for the class to see clearly and could be mounted on the wall in an accessible place;
- **desktop**, which could be either laminated tracks or lines on which children draw and write with water-based pens, or photocopied sheets which they can use like any other worksheet.

Floor tracks: mark these out with masking tape on the back of a length of transparent plastic carpet protector. If numbers are needed, you can stick them under the plastic with Blu-Tack®, or children can place numbers in the squares and move them around as necessary. This track can easily be rolled up and stored or safely left out to be used informally by children at other times. You could also use carpet tiles, each with a number stuck on. Children can physically move these round to get them in order, and they can be stacked when not in use. Alternatively, you could chalk the track directly on the floor.

Floor lines: stick a line of masking tape and markers to carpet protector as above or, for a quick, temporary solution, stick masking tape, or draw with chalk, directly on the floor. *It is important with young children that the markers are spaced regularly.*

Demonstration tracks can be made by joining together numeral cards or writing numbers on strips of squared paper. You could also use a 'washing line' with numbers pegged to it or, to make it easier for small fingers to manipulate, with numbers on folded cards that can be hooked over the line. Such tracks have the advantage that the numbers are easily moved and highly visible.

Demonstration lines: it is probably better to use a commercially produced one, but for some purposes (for example, an unnumbered line with 30 intervals in the activity 'Snake pits') it could be sufficient to draw a line on the board or OHP.

Desktop tracks can be made from the photocopiable *Number lines 1, 2* and *3* provided at the back of this book.

Desktop lines, numbered or unnumbered, can also be made from the photocopiable sheets provided (see page 115). You could use different coloured highlighter pens to colour the decades.

Other equipment

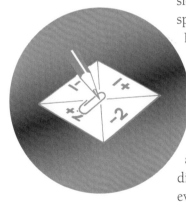

Number cards and **numerals** are needed for many activities. These can be bought, or are easily made by writing on card or blank postcards. It is useful to have sets of 0–10, 0–20, 0–30 cards as well as 0–100. You can also make sets in other number scripts (see page 10).

Dice and spinners can usually be interchanged, but sometimes you will want to choose a spinner: a 1–9 spinner is easy to make, whereas nine-sided dice don't exist. The activities in this book call for dice and spinners with a variety of markings: 1–6, 0–9, numerals, dots or words. Rolling the dice on a cloth-lined tray or lid makes the activity less noisy and more contained.

Commercially produced spinners can be altered with labels as necessary, or you and the children can make your own. A simple, temporary spinner can be made from a sheet of paper with numerals or words written on, and a paper clip held in place by a pencil point as the pointer. You can easily make your own six-sided dice with blank dice or wooden cubes and indelible pens, although unless these are evenly weighted they will not roll fairly. When dice with more sides are specified you will need to use commercially produced ones.

Tokens such as stand-up figures drawn (or cut from magazines and pasted) onto card, or beads, cubes, buttons and so on are useful for games of many kinds.

Laminating, or other clear protective covering, allows water-based felt-tipped pens to be used for recording and then wiped off. (Pens specially designed for this purpose are by far the most satisfactory to use, as they show up well and wipe off cleanly.) Damp and dry cloths are useful for wiping: damp to remove the marks, and dry so the item can be used again immediately. You could use two colours of cloth – blue for damp and yellow for dry, perhaps.

Equipment suppliers

Number cards and blank cards, number fans, counters, play people

Equipment like this is readily available from the major suppliers.
BEAM sells:

- small 0–9 number cards (20 sets to a pack) and more substantial 0–100 cards (one set in a box)
- 0–9 number fans which can be used to display single digits or two-digit numbers
- counters with 1–10 stickers (100 counters in a pack)

Dice and spinners

NES Arnold sells various dice, including 'giant' and 'jumbo' ones that are good for whole class activities.

BEAM sells:

- a wide range of numbered dice, including 1–6 dot dice and 1–6, 0–9, 1–12 and 1–20 numeral dice
- blank dice and stickers with which to number them
- a set of four spinners (numerals 0–6, 0–10, 0–20 and 1–6 dots)

Counting sticks

Philip and Tacey sells a 1 m counting stick divided in 4, 10 and 100 sections on different faces; the 100-section face is numbered in tens at every tenth marker.

Floor tracks

Hope Education sells rubber mats numbered 0–10 that would make a good number track, although you might need to renumber the 0 as 'start'.

Philip and Tacey sells interlocking 0–9 floor tiles 0–9 that would make a good number track, although you might need to renumber the 0 as 10, and add a 'start'.

If you want to buy number tracks for children to walk along, avoid those where the spaces are too small for a child's foot – or restrict their use to 'walking' toy animals and vehicles along them.

Floor lines

These are best made yourself. Most commercially produced lines which are currently available look more like tracks than lines, but include a zero, which is confusing for children. (However, you could change the zero to 'start' and use these 'lines' as number tracks.)

Demonstration lines

LDA sells large lines, over 9 m long, numbered in ones from −20 to +100.

BEAM sells:

- a 2 m line with 100 intervals: on one side every fifth marker is numbered in fives from 0 to 100; the other side is unnumbered

Desktop tracks

BEAM sells:

- sets of ten number tracks, 60 cm long, numbered 0–20 on one side and unnumbered on the other

Desktop lines

Several suppliers offer desktop lines. For example, Philip and Tacey sells lines numbered to 10 and 20, as well as rubber stamps for making your own.

BEAM sells:

- individual lines with 30 intervals, 1 m long, numbered 0–30 on one side and unnumbered on the other
- individual lines with 100 intervals, 1 m long, numbered 0–100 on one side and unnumbered on the other
- desktop lines 28 cm long, (pack of 50 comprising ten each of: 0–30 numbered in ones, 0–100 numbered in fives, 50–150 numbered in fives, 0–1000 numbered in fifties, −50 to +50 numbered in fives)

Pens

BEAM sells:

- packs of ten water-based pens for use on all BEAM number lines – write on and wipe off

Contact information

Hope Education
tel 08702 412308
fax 0800 929139
email orders@hope-education.co.uk
website www.hope-education.co.uk

NES Arnold
tel 0870 600 0192
fax 01530 418181
email enquiries@nesarnold.co.uk
website www.nesarnold.co.uk

LDA
tel 01945 463441
fax 01945 587361
email ldamarketing@tribune.com
website www.instructionalfair.co.uk

Philip and Tacey
tel 01264 332171
fax 01264 361171
email sales@philipandtacey.co.uk
website www.philipandtacey.co.uk

BEAM: see back cover for contact information

Starters

Objectives and resources

★ recognise numerals 1 to 10 and order a given set of numbers

- washing line and pegs
- 1–10 number cards

★ recognise numerals 1 to 10 and order a given set of numbers

- 1–10 number cards

★ count up to 10

- floor 0–10 number track with 'start' before the 1

CLASS

Washing line

Give out the cards and invite children to come up and peg their numbers on the line in order.

Developments

Peg up the 1 and talk about where the other numbers belong.

Deliberately get two numbers the wrong way round then challenge children to spot the mistake.

Miss out a number for children to spot.

CLASS

Children line

Give out the cards to some of the children then, with the watching children, help the card holders to put themselves in order in a line.

Developments

Ask children to change places with those holding cards.

> *Lily, go and take over the number that is one more than 3.*

> *Yasmin, you can hold any number between 2 and 7.*

The watching children close their eyes and one of the number track children hides their card. Everyone opens their eyes and says which number is missing.

Again everyone else closes their eyes but this time two number track children swap their cards. The rest of the class must then spot which they are.

CLASS

Claps

Clap your hands up to ten times and ask a child to do a step along the number track for each beat. The rest of the class can show the number of beats with their fingers and check that this is the same as the number the child is standing on.

Development

Show a number card and, with the children, clap that many times.

* recognise numerals 1 to 10 and order a given set of numbers

• desktop 1–10 number track (*Number line 1*)

Jigsaws

Cut up a number track for each pair and challenge them to put it back together again.

Developments

Use number tracks to 20 or 30.

Cut up two tracks and mix up the pieces, then challenge the children to make two tracks out of the pieces.

Blank out some of the numbers before cutting up the track. As well as putting the track back together, the children must write the missing numbers.

* say and use the number names in order in familiar contexts forwards and back

• demonstration 1–10 number track
• plastic animals or picture cards

Number rhymes

Sing or say a number rhyme with the children which involves counting on or back in ones, for example, 'Five Little Froggies'. Model with fingers and on the number track what happens to the numbers in the rhyme.

> *'Five little froggies sat on a well.' Can you show me five fingers? ... And who can point to the 5 on the number track? Who would like to come and put out five frogs, one on each square?*

> *'One jumped down and down she fell.'*

(Remove the fifth frog from the track.)

> *So how many froggies were left sitting on the well? ... Show me with your fingers. How many frogs are left?*

* understand and use the vocabulary of ordering and comparing numbers

• demonstration 1–30 number track

Voting

Encourage a democratic classroom by asking children to vote on issues such as which story to have at story time or which game to play in PE (but do make sure the minorities also sometimes get their choice). Record the number of votes on the number track and discuss the results.

> *Do more children want* The Enormous Turnip *or* The Cat in the Hat? *How many more?*

Developments

Use a number track to compare other small numbers, for example:
- the number of pigeons, blackbirds and robins seen in the park
- the numbers of children wearing trainers, sandals and buckled shoes
- how many people come to school by car, bus, taxi and on foot.

Objectives and resources

★ count up to 10 and understand the vocabulary of comparing

- demonstration 0–10 number line, with pen
- drum
- chime bar

CLASS **Drumbeats and chimes**

Beat the drum steadily about seven times, and then hit the chime bar about six times. Ask:

Were there more drumbeats or more chimes?

Show children how to keep a tally of sounds on the number line by drawing a step for each sound, drumbeats above the line and chimes below.

Now it's easy to tell, isn't it?

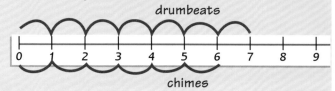

★ know and read the number names to 30 and order them

- demonstration 0–30 number line

CLASS **Cover up**

Cover up one or more numbers with your fingers or large counters. Ask children what is hidden.

Development
Give pairs of children copies of 0–30 number lines with some numbers blanked out. They fill in the blanks.

★ count 'objects' to 30, use and understand the vocabulary of comparing, and understand subtraction as 'difference'

- demonstration 0–50 number line, with pen

CLASS **Roll call**

Count how many children are in class today and ask one of the children to find that number on the line and put a ring around it. Compare today's number with yesterday's.

Are there more children here today, or fewer, or the same number? How many fewer?

Development
Record and compare other numbers, for example, how many 5 year olds there are and how many 6 year olds.

★ understand and use the vocabulary of estimation

- demonstration 0–100 number line
- calculator

CLASS **What's half?**

Choose a number under 100, such as 66. Ask:

What number is about half of 66? Have a look at the number line then find an approximate answer.

Check by dividing 66 by 2 on the calculator. You can invite children to do this.

- ★ understand and use the vocabulary of comparison and understand subtraction as 'difference'

- demonstration 0–20 number line
- felt-tipped pens
- 0–20 number cards

Green or blue?

Divide the class into two teams, green and blue. Ask a representative from each team to choose a number below 20, and ring that number on the line using the appropriate colour of pen. Pick a number card and read it out. Ask:

> *Is the card number closer to the green team's number or the blue team's?*

Underline the card number on the line and invite the children to help you count the steps between that number and the green number, and between that number and the blue number. Whichever team is closer to the target number wins the card.

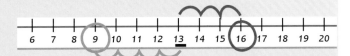

Teams choose a new number each and the winning team is the first to collect, say, five cards.

- ★ order numbers and compare

- desktop 0–30 number lines
- 0–30 number cards

What's my number?

Select at random one of the number cards but do not let the children see the value. Children take turns to suggest a number. Say whether your number is greater or smaller than theirs.

> *My number is greater than 6.*

> *You know my number is greater than 6, so is 5 a good number to choose next?*

Children keep on suggesting numbers, and use their number lines to help them work out v your number is.

> If 6 is too small and 8 is too big, it must be 7.

Development
Invite a child to come to the front, select a card and respond to the suggestions.

- ★ count in twos, fives and tens

- demonstration 0–100 number line, with pen

Kangaroo jumps

When children are still getting used to the idea of equal jumps on a number line, use the idea of a kangaroo. Tiny kangaroos take one step at a time: 1, 2, 3, …

A small kangaroo might jump in twos: 2, 4, 6, 8, …
A medium kangaroo might jump in fives: 5, 10, 15, …
A big kangaroo might jump in tens: 10, 20, 30, …

Ask different children to demonstrate.

Objectives and resources

* ★ order numbers to 20 and write the numerals

* demonstration unnumbered line with 20 intervals (*Number line 10*), with pen
* 0–20 number cards

* ★ add or subtract a single digit to/from a multiple of 10
* ★ make general statements
* ★ double single digits

* spinner showing the numerals 1–9
* demonstration line with 100 intervals numbered in fives, with pen

* ★ recognise and understand $\frac{1}{2}$ as a fraction

* unnumbered floor line with 11 intervals (chalk on the floor will do)
* number cards with whole and half numbers to 10 ($0, \frac{1}{2}, 1, 1\frac{1}{2}, 2, \ldots$)

CLASS

Point and tell

Write in 0, 10 and 20 at the appropriate markers. Hold up one of the number cards and ask a child to read the number; ask another child to point to where that number belongs on the line and then to write it in. Continue like this until all the markers are numbered.

Development
Use some 0–100 cards and a line numbered in fives.

CLASS

Give and take

Ring any multiple of 10 on the line (for example, 30) then invite one of the children to roll the dice and read out the number. Ask the class to predict where you will land if you take that many steps forwards, and the same number of steps backwards, from the ringed number.

Draw the steps and underline the numbers you landed on, then ask:

> *What is the difference between the two underlined numbers?*

dice number	difference
3	6
2	4
5	10

Draw the children's attention to the fact that the difference is double the dice number and discuss whether this is true whatever the starting number.

CLASS or GROUP

Fraction floor line

Ask children to put the whole numbers at the appropriate markers. Then talk about the half numbers and ask the children to help place these cards too.

> *Now I have some more number cards to put out. These show the half numbers. They are like your age when you are three and a half, or six and a half.*

Finally, invite the children to take turns to start at 0 and count along the line in halves.

> *Sanjit, count along five halves. ... What number has Sanjit landed on? ... $2\frac{1}{2}$?*

- ★ count in tens and ones

- two dice showing numerals 1, 1, 2, 2, 3, 3
- two spinners showing 0–9
- desktop line with 100 intervals numbered in fives (*Number line 7*)
- a supply of fir-cones
- felt-tipped pens

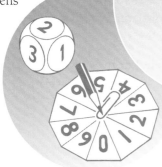

PAIRS

Fir-cones for further

Each child has a dice and spinner; the dice indicates how many jumps of ten they will make from 0 and the spinner indicates the number of extra single steps to take. Both children roll their dice and spin their spinner. They then predict who will go further.

The child who thinks they will go further takes a fir-cone. They then both draw their jumps and steps and write in the number where they land. If the child with the fir-cone was right in their prediction, they keep it.

> Three jumps of ten and three steps. I think I'll go further.

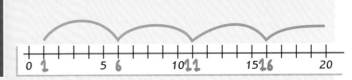

Both children then start again from zero.

CLASS or GROUP

- ★ describe and extend simple number sequences, counting on in fives

- demonstration line with 100 intervals numbered in fives, with pen

Drawing jumps from 1

Draw a series of five-jumps from 1 and ask a child to write on the line the numbers where you land. Ask:

> *1, 6, 11, 16, 21, ... What do you think will come next ...? What makes you think that?*

Record the numbers in a list and look at the patterns in the results.

Can you predict what the next number will be?

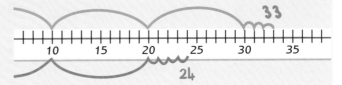

1	6
11	16
21	

Development
Draw jumps of ten from 1 or 2 or 4.
Draw jumps of five from 2 or 3 or 4.

CLASS or GROUP

- ★ describe and extend simple number sequences, counting on in steps of two, three, four and five

- demonstration unnumbered line with 50 or 100 intervals, with pen
- calculator

Jump patterns

Choose a number from 2 to 5 and ask a child to make jumps that size from 0 on a calculator; they call out the numbers shown. Another child writes these numbers on the line.

Look at the patterns in the results with the group. See if they can predict what the next number will be.

23

Objectives and resources

★ describe and extend
number sequences

★ find the sum of two
two-digit numbers

• 0–9 number cards
• pens and paper

★ count and extend a number
sequence
★ understand multiplication
as repeated addition

• board and marker

CLASS or GROUP

Imaginary number lines

Ask children to close their eyes and imagine the numbers in order. Tell them there is no right and wrong way to do this; you are simply interested in what they see. Ask:

What do your numbers look like? ... Are they in line? A straight line? A wiggly one?

What numbers can you see? Is there a 0? And a 1? And a 10? A 20? Are your numbers coloured? Are some bigger than others?

If you walk along your line away from 0 or 1, what happens? Can you still see the numbers clearly?

How far does your line go? To 100? Or more? If you were standing at the 100 point on the line and looked ahead what would you see? And what if you looked back?

Can you continue your line for ever?

PAIRS

Make a sum

Children pick four cards and arrange those numbers to make two two-digit numbers, for example, 38 and 54. Ask them to find the sum of these numbers using an empty number line.

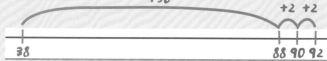

They then rearrange the numbers to make a different pair of numbers, say 84 and 35, and find the sum of these.

Which arrangement gives you the biggest sum?

Development
Find the difference between the pairs of numbers.

CLASS

Counting patterns

Draw a series of equal jumps on an empty number line (from 0 or another number), and label each landing place. Ask the children what size of jump you are using.

9, 12, 15. What comes next? ... What is the size of the jumps?

★ count on in ones, twos, fives, tens and twenties

• bag of coins (1p to 20p, but only one 50p piece)
• board and marker

CLASS
and
PAIRS

Collecting money

Invite children one at a time to pick a coin out of the bag and tell the rest of the class how much it is worth. Keep track of the total by drawing jumps on an empty number line.

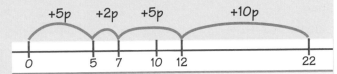

As you do this, encourage prediction.

> *I'm on 54p and Sandra has pulled out a 5p. Where will another 5p take me to? ...*

Tell the children they must make the total up to £1 using the exact coin.

> *I'm on 82p and Olu has pulled out a 20p. Can we use it? ... Why not? ... We'll have to pull out another coin and try again.*

Check the result by arranging the coins in order of value, largest first, and counting along another empty line.

Pairs of children can then repeat the activity, taking turns to pick a coin.

Development

Start at 100 (£1) with a bag of coins worth exactly £1 and move back towards 0. When children reach 0 all the coins should have been used up; if they haven't, this is a sign that they have gone wrong in their calculations.

★ add 9 or 11

• dice (or spinner) showing +9, +9, +9, +11, +11, +11
• pens and paper

FOURS

Racing to 90

Divide the children into two teams. Each team draws an empty number line. Then, starting at 0, they take turns to roll the dice and add 9 or 11.

Encourage children to predict where their moves will end up. Remind them they can add either number by making a jump of ten and then adjusting the answer.

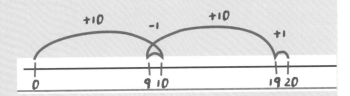

> *Yemi is going to draw a ten-jump from 9, then go forwards a step. So what number will she land on?*

The first team past 90 wins the game.

section 1 Numbers and the number system

Counting, comparing and ordering

Secret steps

Objectives

★ say and use the number names in order
★ count reliably
★ count on from any small number

You need

- 1–5 number cards
- floor 1–10 number track with 'start' before the 1

for each pair or small group:
- desktop 1–10 number tracks (*Number line 2*) with 'start' before the 1
- counters or play people
- 1–5 number cards
- spinner showing numerals 1–5

TEACHING POINT

You can count on from any number.

Children play a game where one child has a card showing a secret number and takes steps accordingly; the other children work out the secret number.

Although this game is played on a number track, it could also be played on a number line.

Working with the children

Learning the game

Ask the children to sit beside the floor number track. One child gets up and stands on Start. Give this child a number card and ask them to look at it (and whisper the number to you) but not to let the others know what the number is.

Now tell the child to take that many steps along the track while the others count the steps. (Show how to make each step with both feet. This means that when the child stops they will know what number they are on – which is not always the case if they use left and right feet alternately.)

The observers then hold up their fingers to show how many steps were taken.

Talk about how the number on the square where the child has ended up matches the number on the card they were given.

Steps from other numbers

After one or two goes like this, ask the child who is doing the steps to start at a different number (not more than 5, though). As this child takes her steps along the line, the rest of the children should count the steps altogether and hold up their fingers to show how many steps she took.

Talk about why this time the number where the child has ended up is not the same as the number on the card.

When the children are used to the activity, ask them to count the steps silently, in their heads or on their fingers.

Children working independently

The children can play in pairs or small groups using play people on a desktop 1–10 number track.

Give them a spinner showing the numbers 1 to 5 to determine the starting number, and number cards 1 to 5 to tell them how many steps to make their play person take.

Encourage prediction – where do they think their person will end up each time?

Gathering the children together

Hold up a number card below 5 and ask the children to imagine standing on that number on the number track. Now show another card, or hold up a number of fingers, and ask them to try and work out in their heads where they would end up if they took that many steps forwards from the starting number.

Children can display the answer:
- with number cards
- by holding up fingers
- by drawing the answer in the air

or you can ask a volunteer to tell you the answer.

Variations

◆ Play without a track. One child simply takes steps according to the secret number, while the others work out what the number is.

◆ Children start at 10 and take steps back toward Start. This variation is important, as too often children get experience of counting forwards and adding, but not of the opposite, subtracting and going backwards.

Challenges

◆ Children take the number of steps on their card plus one more. The others must work out the number on the card. Extend to one less than the number on their card.

◆ Children use a 1–20 or 30 number track and cards with higher numbers. They can start from any number up to 10.

◆ Use a 1–20 number track and start all steps from 10. Talk about what happens.

Three steps from 10 takes you to 13, and five steps from 10 takes you to 15. That is the same as the number of steps you took but with a 1 in front. That 1 really means ten.

Racing to 10

CLASS
then **PAIRS**

Objectives

* ★ say and use the number names in order
* ★ recognise zero
* ★ count on from any small number

Children practise making and counting steps on a floor number line. This is an important skill as children need to learn to count the movement forward (or back) rather than the markers. Counting steps gives an accurate answer, whereas counting markers does not.

They then play a racing game in teams which gives them practical experience of 'counting on' on a number line.

You need

* giant dice or spinner showing just 0 and 1
* floor 0–10 number line with long markers
* 0–10 number cards

  for each pair:
* desktop 0–10 number line (you could use a section of *Number line 5*)
* counters or play people
* dice or spinner showing just 0 and 1

  for each child:
* number fan (optional)

Working with the children

Teach children to make each step on the line with both feet. This means they can stop anywhere on the line and know what number they are on – which is not always the case if they use left and right feet alternately.

Invite one child at a time to practise taking steps along the line, from 0 forwards to 10 and then back to 0. Ask the rest of the children to count the steps out loud as they are made.

TEACHING POINT

On a number line, you count the steps you make, not the places you stand on.

Divide the children into two teams. One child in each team stands on 0 (which is why the markers need to be long). The teams take turns to roll the dice and instruct their representative on the line to take that many steps forwards.

Whichever team reaches 10 first wins the game.

Children working independently

The children play in pairs using counters or play people on a desktop line with a spinner or dice showing numbers 1 and 0.

Encourage prediction: where do they think their person will end up each time?

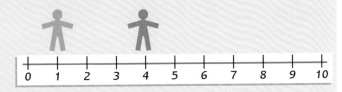

Gathering the children together

Hold up a number card from 0 to 10 and ask the children to imagine standing on that number on the number line. Ask:

> *Where would you move to if you rolled a dice and it showed 1? ... What if you rolled zero?*

Children can display the answer:
- with number fans
- by holding up fingers
- by drawing the answer in the air

or you can ask a volunteer to tell you the answer.

Variations

◆ *Number line 4* provides a number ladder from 0 to 10 which can be used for this game or, if you have a wooden number ladder, children can use pegs with pictures of people glued to them as the tokens.

◆ Children start at 10 and race back to 0. This variation is important, as too often children get experience of counting forwards and adding, but not of the opposite, subtracting and going backwards to 0.

Simplification

◆ Some children may find it easier to learn the mechanics of taking steps on a line with markers but no numbers. This will allow them to concentrate on counting their steps, without being distracted by numbers.

Challenges

◆ Children use a dice or spinner that shows 0, 1 and 2. They must throw the right number at the end.

◆ Children use a 0–20 or 30 number line and a dice that shows 1, 2 and 3.

◆ Children use a dice showing 0, +1, +2, −1, −2 so that they go back as well as forward.

CLASS
then **PAIRS**

Objectives

★ write whole numbers to 100 in figures
★ order whole numbers to 100, and position them on a number line

You need

- board and marker
- demonstration line with 100 intervals numbered in fives, with pen
- 0–9 dice or number cards
- arrow cards

for each pair:
- desktop unnumbered line with 30 intervals (*Number line 9*), with pen

TEACHING POINT

Every number has its own special position in the number sequence.

Two digits are arranged to make two different numbers, then children locate these on a line where the multiples of five are written in: 0, 5, 10, 15, 20 and so on.

Providing a few key numbers helps children find their way about the line, and provides clues as to where the other numbers they are given belong.

Working with the children

Roll two 0–9 dice (or draw two number cards at random) and write up the numbers on the board. Discuss with the children how to arrange these to make a two-digit number, and ask them to help you find the place on the demonstration line where that number belongs. Invite a child to come up to the line and write it in.

Establish that the same two digits can be rearranged to make another number. Again, ask the children to find the place on the demonstration line where it belongs and invite a child to write the number in.

Continue rolling the dice (or return the cards, shuffle and draw again), making two numbers (unless you roll a double, such as two sevens) and writing them in on the line. At some point you will roll a zero, and will need to introduce the idea that you can still make two different numbers.

For example, 3 and 0 can make 30, and can also make 03 (which is 3). You may want to demonstrate this on a tens and ones board or abacus. Three beads on the tens wire and none on the ones represents 30. No beads on the tens wire and three on the ones can be represented by the same two digits, 0 and 3.

The number is 53. Where do the fifties come on the line?

I can make 48 and 84. Which of them is the bigger number? Which is smaller?

The number is 29. Where on the line does 29 come? Do I need to count on from 20 to find it?

We had 65 last time; now I've got 66. What is a quick way to find where 66 goes?

Children working independently

Children work in pairs using desktop unnumbered lines with 30 intervals. Give each pair a different multiple of 10 to write at the first marker and help them to work out which other multiples of 10 will go on their line and to write them at the correct place.

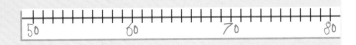

Continue rolling the two dice and writing the digits up on the board. Encourage children to work out for themselves which two numbers the digits can make, but provide support if necessary. Each pair checks whether either or both numbers belong on their segment of line and, if so, they locate the right place and write it in.

Continue until some pairs have written in ten or so numbers, then stop. Ask the children to write in all the missing numbers on their lines.

Gathering the children together

Rub out the numbers on the demonstration line. Use arrow cards to create various two-digit numbers (or ask children to do this) and each time write in the number on the line – but tell the children you may be putting it in the wrong place. Challenge them to notice when you are making a deliberate mistake.

Kav has used the 40 and 5 arrow cards. That makes 54. Am I right?

The number is 89. That comes just before 90. Am I right?

section 1

Variations

◆ Write up three or more numbers and invite children to put them in order, using a numbered line to check.

◆ Write up two numbers on the board and ask children to tell you which is the larger and which is smaller. Then ask them to tell you some numbers which come between.

◆ Two children share a number line numbered in fives, but each has a pen in a different colour. They take turns to roll two 0–9 dice, arrange the digits to make a two-digit number, and write this in on the line (or if they make a multiple of 5, they just ring the number). The first player to get three numbers in their colour wins the game.

◆ Children write in a sequence of numbers on an unnumbered line but swap two of the numbers around. They challenge others to work out which two numbers were swapped.

Simplifications

◆ Provide lines with the multiples of 10 already written in.

◆ Provide lines with multiples of 5 already written in.

Make your own 0–10 number line

CLASS
then **PAIRS**

Objectives

★ understand and use the vocabulary of comparing and ordering numbers
★ read and write the numerals to 10
★ understand and use vocabulary related to length

You need

• board and marker
• counting stick (optional)

for each pair:
• paper and pencils

Children put the missing numbers on a line which shows only 0 and 10.

This is a valuable activity which helps children develop their own mental model of numbers in order. A version with higher numbers appears on p54 and a version with fractions on p60.

The activity also prepares children for using an 'empty' number line, which is a valuable tool for assisting with mental calculations. (For more on the empty number line in general see p7.)

Working with the children

Draw a line on the board. Mark starting and end points on the line, and number these 0 and 10.

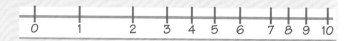

Ask children to tell you the numbers that belong in the rest of the line and mark these on. Start with 1, then 2, and so on, but make the intervals too big, so that later numbers are squashed.

Now discuss the need to make the intervals between the numbers equal, as far as possible. Rub out the ones you have done and start again.

TEACHING POINT

●

The numbers on a number line should all be in order.

What number shall we put in first? ... The one in the middle? Why will that help? ... Can you come and mark it in?

Where does 4 belong? And 6? And 1?

What numbers need to fit in between the 1 and the 4?

Talk about spaces between the markers needing to be the same size. Ask whether there is room for the 2 and the 3. If necessary, rub out the 1 and 4 and move them along so there is space for the other numbers.

Children working independently

When the line is complete, count along with the children, then rub out all the numbers except the 0 and the 10.

In pairs, the children draw their own lines. They put 0 and 10 at each end, then discuss together where to put the markers and numbers.

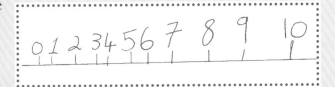

Gathering the children together

Hold up one of the children's number lines, hiding a numeral with your finger or thumb. Ask what the missing number is.

Hide two numerals and ask what they are.

Hold up a counting stick. Say that one end is 0 and the other 10. Indicate a place on the stick and ask what number belongs there.

Variations

Simplification

◆ Give children a number line to copy.

◆ Give children an unnumbered line (with markers but no numbers) to fill in.

◆ Provide number cards to put in order, as a reminder.

Challenges

◆ Children make lines showing only odd or only even numbers. Or make lines showing every number, but use colours to differentiate odd from even.

◆ Children make a number line on blank paper to 20 or 30.

◆ Children turn over random number cards and write them on an empty line.

section **2 Numbers and the number system**

Estimating and rounding

Guess!

CLASS
then **PAIRS**

Objectives

★ give a sensible estimate of a number of objects
★ compare two numbers and say which is more/less
★ understand and use the vocabulary of comparing and ordering numbers

You need

• plastic jar (or large transparent bag) of up to twenty objects, such as ping pong balls, conkers, …
• demonstration 1–20 number track (pen optional)
• Post-it notes or similar (optional)

for each pair:
• desktop 0–20 number track (*Number line 3*), with pen
• cubes (or miniature teddies, cars, animals, shells, …)
• smaller transparent bag with seal or tie

Children estimate how many objects there are in a jar and record their estimates on a number track. They then count the objects and mark the actual number on the number track. (Names can be written directly onto a laminated track or onto Post-it notes.)

This provides an opportunity for much discussion about the order, and relative size, of numbers, as well as providing practice in the skills of estimation.

Working with the children

Show the children the jar (or bag) containing the objects. Hand it round the class and invite suggestions as to how many objects it contains.

Ask each child in turn to commit themselves to a number and record this on the number track.

Before you count the objects, talk about:
● which guess (estimate) is highest and which is lowest
● the approximate difference between the highest and lowest guesses (you may not want to work this out exactly)
● any guesses which are approximately halfway between the highest and lowest guesses.

Empty out the jar and encourage the children to count the objects with you. Record the actual number of objects on the number track and talk about:
● which guess (estimate) was closest
● which guesses were not so close
● who guessed there were more objects than the jar contained, and who guessed there were fewer

and possibly:
● the difference between the closest guess and the actual number

TEACHING POINT

●

You can use a number track to compare numbers.

Children working independently

Work with one pair to demonstrate the following activity, before the rest of the class try it for themselves.

Give the pair a 1–20 number track, a plastic bag and about 20 cubes or other objects. One child closes their eyes while the other one counts some of the cubes into the bag, seals it up and lays it on the table, then rings that number on their number track and turns the track face down. (If the track is not laminated they can use Post-it notes.)

The first child looks at the bag without touching it, estimates the number of objects it contains, and announces their guess.

Both children look at the number track, ring the number estimated by the first child, and compare the two numbers. Encourage them to talk about which number is greater, the estimate or the actual number. Is there a big difference or was it a close guess?

Then they empty the bag, wipe the numbers off, and swap roles.

Gathering the children together

Hold up one of the children's bag of objects and invite the class to estimate the number of its contents. Ask the owner of the bag how many it actually contains and then ask who guessed more than that and who guessed less. Refer to a number track as necessary to check which numbers are more or less than the estimate.

Repeat this with other bags.

Variations

◆ Use carrier bags and items of shopping.

◆ Hide a number of cubes in a yoghurt pot with a lid. Children shake the pot and listen carefully, as well as judging how it feels in their hands. Then they make their estimate.

Challenges

◆ Start with a blank number track. Children write in the number of their estimate on the correct space on the track.

◆ To challenge children's skills in estimation, give them a mixture of objects of slightly different sizes.

◆ Children estimate a quantity which is likely to involve simple fractions (for example, how many cups of juice there are in a jug). They will need to use a number *line*, where numbers such as 'three and a bit' or 'one and a half' can be marked between the whole numbers.

Round it

Objectives

★ know what each digit in a two-digit number represents
★ round numbers to the nearest 10

You need

- demonstration 0–100 number line
- 0–9 number cards or number fan or two 0–9 dice

for each pair:
- desktop 0–100 number line (*Number line 6*)
- two 0–9 dice
- felt-tipped pens in two different colours

Children make a two-digit number then round this up or down to the nearest ten and mark it on the number line. Because the numbers on the line are equally spaced, children can use visual clues to decide whether they should round up or down, and can see that numbers such as 15 and 25 are actually halfway between the nearest tens-numbers.

Children have to choose which way round to use their two digits to make a number. This reinforces their understanding of what each digit represents.

Working with the children

Spend a few minutes with the children looking at numbers on the number line and choosing numbers to round up or down to the nearest multiple of 10. Remind children that by convention numbers ending in 5 are rounded up.

Ask children to suggest two single-digit numbers and write these on the board, for example, 3 and 7, and ask which two-digit numbers can be made from them.

> *If we make 37, and we want to round it to the nearest 10, do we round up or down? ... And if we make it 73, do we round up or down?*

Repeat with other digits if necessary, then children can move on to playing the game.

Children working independently

Playing in pairs, each child chooses a different colour pen. They take turns to:

- roll both dice, and say the numbers
- choose how to arrange the dice-numbers to make a two-digit number
- round that number to the nearest ten
- write their initial by that number on the line

I've got an 8 and a 2. I'm going to make 82 and round it to 80.

F

77 78 79 80 81 82 83 84 85 86 87 88 89 90 91 92 93 94

The other player should check that the numbers have been dealt with correctly, and that no cheating (whether deliberate or accidental) takes place.

Only two initials can be written by a number. (One player may write their initial twice by the same number.) If a player makes a number which already has two initials by it, they miss that turn. The game ends when one of the players has written their initial six times.

Gathering the children together

Play a quick game with the class. Everybody chooses a multiple of 10 from the number line (including 0 and 100) and tells their partner what number they have chosen.

Now roll two 0–9 dice and arrange them to form a two-digit number (or pick two digit cards from a pack, or make a number with a number fan). Ask the class to tell you what multiple of 10 to round it up or down to. Any child who had picked that multiple of 10 wins a point (or can go out to play, or have first go on the computer ...).

Variations

◆ Round numbers up or down to the nearest multiple of 5.

◆ Link the activity to rounding of measurements: talk about when it is and is not appropriate to round them up or down.

Simplifications

◆ Help children to ring all the multiples of 10 on the line.

◆ Restrict the dice to the numbers 0, 1, 2 and 3, and use a number line to 30.

Challenges

◆ Pairs or small groups can play without a number line. They roll the dice and make a two-digit number as before, and round this up or down to the nearest 10 (or 5). After ten rounds they add up the rounded numbers to find their total score.

ISObel	Sunil	Christy
30 → 30	11 → 10	40 → 40
73 → 70	74 → 70	61 → 60

◆ Children can use three dice, and make three-digit numbers, then round these to the nearest 10, 50 or 100. There is no need for a number line at this stage.

41

School fair

Objectives

★ give a sensible estimate of a number of objects
★ write whole numbers to 100
★ estimate lengths, masses and capacities

You need

• plastic jar of sweets, or cake with currants, or similar
• demonstration line with 100 intervals numbered in fives, with pens
• demonstration 0–100 number line (optional)

for each group:
• desktop line with 100 intervals numbered in fives (*Number line 7*), with pens

Children estimate how many objects there are in a jar or currants in a cake, then record their estimates on a number line. They later make other estimates involving measures.

The number line has 100 markers but only the fives and tens are numbered, so children must work out where on the line to write their name and also write in the number for that marker. This demands that children think about the structure of the number system, as well as providing practice in the skills of estimation.

Note that this activity does not follow the usual lesson format.

At any time

At the school fair (or just for fun) fill a jar with sweets (or bake a cake with a set number of currants). Invite suggestions as to how many items are in the cake or jar (there should be fewer than 100).

Each child records their guess on the number line. If they choose a number other than a multiple of 5 they should write in the number by the appropriate marker.

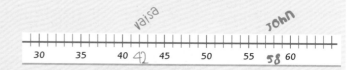

The closest estimate wins the sweets or cake.

Class activity

Follow this up with a class activity, which can be repeated daily for a while.

Show the children something else you want them to estimate, for example, a bucket (how many potfuls of sand will it hold?), a rubber ball (how many shells does it balance?), a stick of cubes (how many cubes does it contain?) or a broom handle (how many handspans long is it?).

A group of children share a desktop line with 100 intervals numbered only in fives. Each child in the

TEACHING POINT

If some numbers are written in on a line with markers, you can work out what the other numbers are.

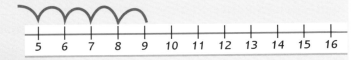

group makes their estimate and records it on the shared line, writing in their name and the number as before.

Now find out the answer together. You could show each step on a separate, numbered line.

```
  ⌢ ⌢ ⌢ ⌢
  5  6  7  8  9  10 11 12 13 14 15 16
```

> It's 9 potfuls so far.

Ask the children to record the actual measurement on their lines. Ask each group in turn to tell you which estimate was closest, and how much it was. The person in each group who was closest wins a point (or earns some benefit such as choosing which game to play).

Variations

◆ If dealing with capacity, present the number line vertically, to make it more like the scale on the side of a measuring jug.

Challenge

◆ Talk about how to record an estimate (or measurement) such as 'five and a bit' or 'ten and a half'. Find a bucket that holds, say, between eight and nine yoghurt pots of water. Ask children to estimate how many pots it will hold and record these, then carry out the actual measurement. Look with the children at the space between 8 and 9 on the line and discuss where and how to record 'eight and a bit'.

Empty number line

X marks the spot

Objectives

★ understand and use the vocabulary of comparing and ordering numbers
★ compare two numbers and say which is more/less
★ estimate lengths

You need

• board and marker
• demonstration number line to at least 20

Children are presented with an empty line showing zero at the start and a multiple of 10 at the end. First, they work out what number belongs halfway, then estimate what numbers belong at other points on the line.

This demands that children think about the order of numbers, as well as providing practice in the skills of estimating lengths.

Note that this activity does not follow the usual lesson format.

Working with the children

Finding the halfway number

Draw a line on the board. Mark a starting point and number it 0; mark an end point, and number it with 10, 20, or any multiple of 10. Then mark the halfway point. Discuss what number might go here (but don't necessarily expect an exact answer).

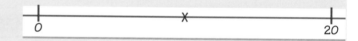

What number do you think the cross might mark?
What number is halfway between 0 and 20?

Now look with the children at a numbered line and agree which number is halfway between 0 and the end number.

What does 'halfway' mean?

Jake says 'halfway' means 'in the middle'. Can you come and point to the middle number between 0 and 20, Jake?

Rub out the cross on your empty number line and draw a marker in its place. Write in the number at this marker.

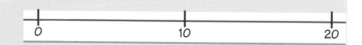

TEACHING POINT

●

If two numbers are written in on the line, you can estimate where other numbers belong.

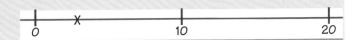

Other points on the line

Draw a cross in a new position and ask:

What number do you think the cross might mark this time? I only want an estimate; it doesn't have to be an exact answer.

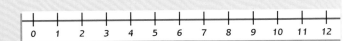

Help children use the evidence provided.

Is the number more or less than 10?

Is it nearer to 0 or to 10?

If the cross marks a number nearer 0 than 10, could it be 6? ... Why not?

Again, look at a numbered line and agree which number, or numbers, the cross might mark.

```
0  1  2  3  4  5  6  7  8  9  10  11  12
```

The number is nearer to 0 than to 10. So it must be less than 5, mustn't it?

Rub out the cross and draw another one. (Don't write in the number, as you did with the halfway mark: it is hard to be precise about what number the cross does represent, and the two end numbers and midway number provide enough clues for the children.) Again discuss what number the cross might represent.

Continue putting the cross in a new position and guessing the number for as long as appropriate.

Variations

◆ Write in numbers at the start and halfway mark. What number belongs at the end?

◆ Use a counting stick. Mark the ends 0 and 100 and work out where numbers such as 10, 20, 50 and 90 belong. (Because the stick has markers, you can work out exactly where these numbers go.) Estimate where intermediate numbers such as 12, 25 or 93 would come.

Simplification

◆ Use a counting stick instead of a line, with 0 at one end and 20 at the other. Because the stick has markers, it is easier to work out exactly where the numbers go.

Challenges

◆ Choose an end number that is not a multiple of 10.

◆ Practise halving by keeping the cross at mid-point, and changing the number at the end point. If appropriate, show children on an overhead calculator how to find half of a number.

◆ Put a number other than 0 at the start of the line. If the first marker is 10 and the end marker is 50, what number comes halfway along? Place a cross somewhere else on the line and ask what number might belong there.

cards / postcards

envelopes

dictionaries

section 3 Numbers and the number system

Number sequences and patterns

Zigzag books

CLASS
then **INDIVIDUALS**
or **PAIRS**

Objectives

★ read and write numerals to 10
★ recognise odd and even numbers
★ order numbers

Children put numbers to 10 in order, then make zigzag number books with one numeral per page. The resulting physical representation shows children very clearly the pattern of odd, even, odd, even, …

You need

• large 1–10 number cards
• washing line and pegs

for each child or pair:
• strip of paper folded concertina-wise to make ten 'pages' (an A4 sheet cut in half lengthwise and stuck end to end makes ten 'pages' almost 6 cm wide)
• felt-tipped pens

TEACHING POINT

●

The pattern of numbers goes: odd, even, odd, even and so on.

Working with the children

Spend a few minutes counting with the children from 1 up to 10 or 20, and then back again.

Now invite ten children to stand up. Give out large number cards, each showing one of the numbers from 1 to 10. Ask the ten children to hold their cards up so they are clearly visible. The children who are sitting down now instruct the children with the number cards where to stand so that they are in a line, with their numbers in order.

Peg these cards up on a washing line as a number track for children to refer to in the work to come.

Children working independently

Give each child (or perhaps pair of children) a strip of paper folded concertina-wise to make ten 'pages'. Ask the children to make this into a zigzag number book showing the numbers 1 to 10, with one numeral to a page.

Remind the children to refer to the numbers on the washing line if they forget the order or orientation of the numbers.

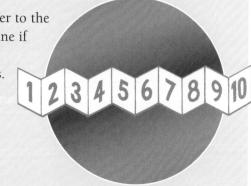

Gathering the children together

Hold up one of the children's zigzag books, facing the children, and turn it slightly so that the odd numbers are visible, but not the even ones.

With the children, recite the sequence of odd numbers to 9. Make sure to use the word 'odd'.

Now turn the book the other way so that the even numbers are visible, and with the children recite the sequence of even numbers to 10. Make sure to use the word 'even'.

The children can then experiment with turning their own books to show the odd and even numbers.

Finally, look at some story books with the children and talk about how the page numbers follow a similar pattern: all the left-hand pages are even and all the right-hand are odd.

Variations

◆ Children can illustrate the number on each page.

◆ Cover up the number on one page and challenge children to tell you what number you are hiding.

◆ A pair of children of differing abilities can work together to make a long zigzag book: one child does the numbers 1 to 10 and the other does the numbers 11 to 20, then they join the two strips together.

Simplification
◆ Children can make books up to just 6.

Challenges
◆ Give children two colours to use alternately; then the odd and even numbers will end up coloured differently.

◆ Children can make zigzag books showing a different number sequence: 11 to 20, multiples of 10, 101 to 110, …

◆ Just talk about what a book with numbers up to 20 would be like.

What's going on?

Objectives

★ count on in steps of three, four and five
★ begin to know the 3, 4 and 5 times tables
★ understand multiplication as repeated addition

You need

• demonstration 0–100 number line, with pen
  or
• OHP and number line at least to 30 on OHT, with pen

for each pair:
• desktop 0–100 number line (*Number line 6*), with pens

The teacher draws jumps in secret from 0, then asks the children to work out the size of jumps by looking at a section of the line only. The children repeat the activity in pairs.

Not being able to see where the first jumps land means the children have to think more about the size of the jumps, focusing their attention on other multiples of the number.

For more on equal jumps see the section 'Calculations: multiplication and division' starting on p83.

Working with the children

On the demonstration line or OHP draw some equal-sized jumps of three or four, starting at 0. Make sure the children can tell you what size the jumps are.

Rub these out and draw a few equal jumps of five from 0, but this time don't let the children see you do it. Show them the number line, but cover up the first decade. Ask:

What size of jump is this? ... How do you know?

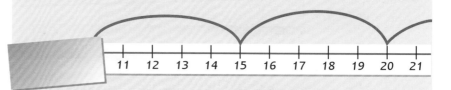

Ask children to predict where the next few jumps in the series will end up, then draw these in and confirm what the correct landing places are. Children repeat with you the sequence of numbers, emphasizing the repeating pattern: 5, 10, 15, 20, 25, 30, ...

Repeat this with jumps of 3 and 4.

Children working independently

In pairs, children take turns to draw their own series of equal jumps from 0 on a 0–100 desktop number line, without their partner seeing. (They could go up to just 40 or 50.) They cover up the first few numbers with

TEACHING POINT

Once you know how numbers work you can continue a number sequence in either direction.

their hand and challenge their partner to work out what size the jumps are. Most children will concentrate on jumps of three, four or five but others may choose higher numbers.

Gathering the children together

Ask two children to stand up with their number line with a series of jumps completed to the end. They show the rest of the class, with their hands (or pieces of paper) covering the first and last decades. The others must work out the size of jump and also predict where the hidden jumps landed.

Repeat with other pairs who have completed their lines with other sizes of jump.

Variations

◆ Copy the landing numbers onto paper and look at the patterns.

5	10
15	20
25	30
35	40

Simplification

◆ Children could work in pairs to draw the lines and then present them to the teacher or another pair to work out, instead of to each other.

Challenge

◆ Draw equal-sized jumps from any number under 10. Keeping the whole of the first decade covered, challenge the children to work out both the size of jump and the starting point.

CLASS
then **PAIRS**

Objectives

★ count on or back in steps of one and jumps of ten from any two-digit number
★ read and write numbers to 100
★ know what each digit in a two-digit number represents

You need

• demonstration line with 100 intervals numbered in fives, with two pens
• dice or spinner showing just 1 and 10

for each pair:
• desktop line with 100 intervals numbered in fives (*Number line 7*), with two pens
• dice or spinner showing just 1 and 10

TEACHING POINT

If you add 10 to a number the ones digit stays the same and the tens digit increases by one.

Children draw jumps of one and ten on a line where only the multiples of 5 are written in. This encourages children to think about the structure of the number system and helps develop their understanding of place value.

It is a good idea, as a preliminary exercise, for children to play a similar game on a fully numbered 100-grid. The experience of moving one and ten spaces on a grid offers a different, and complementary, perspective on how our number system works.

Working with the children

Divide the class into two teams and explain the game. Both teams start at 0 and race to 100, drawing jumps of either one or ten according to the roll of the dice.

Roll the dice for each team in turn and ask representatives from each team to come up and draw the appropriate step or jump, then write in the number where they end up. One team should jump above the line and the other team below.

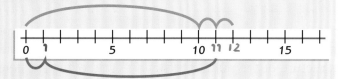

Encourage children to predict where ten-jumps will end up, and to check that they agree with what their representative has drawn.

> *Judit is going to draw a ten-jump from 1. Where should she end? ... Sean thinks it should be 11. Both numbers end in a 1 don't they?*
>
> *Judit, where have you ended? What number belongs there? ... Does everyone agree with that? ... How can we check that she drew the jump the right size?*

At the end of the game, the teams should wait until they throw the right number to reach 100.

Children working independently

In pairs, children now play the game on their desktop lines. Children should both check each time that the jumps have been made the right size.

Gathering the children together

Play a game with two teams again, starting at 100 and moving back towards 0. It is important that children also play the game 'backwards': this gives them practical experience of subtracting 1 and 10 from two-digit numbers.

Variations

◆ Play the same game with calculators instead of a number line. Children each have a calculator and add 10 or 1 to their running total according to the roll of the dice. Encourage prediction.

Simplification
◆ Children play the game on a fully numbered line.

Challenges
◆ Children can add 9 or 11, using dice numbered 0, 1, 9, 10, 10, 11.

◆ Children can start by writing in the 'fives' numbers themselves on an unnumbered line.

◆ Children can play on a line which begins at 50. They race to 150, writing in the correct number wherever they land.

◆ Children can play the game without a number line. They start at 0, and roll the dice to show them how much to add to their score.

Frances	Hussain
0	0
10	10
11	11
12	21
22	31

Make your own 90–120 number line

Children help the teacher extend the number sequence past 100 to 120 and practise counting both forwards and backwards. They then create their own number line from 90 to 120.

This is a valuable activity which helps children focus on how the number sequence develops above 100, and how it is like and unlike the sequence that starts at 0.

Objectives

★ describe and extend number sequences past 100
★ read and write numbers over 100
★ count on and back in ones past 100

You need

• demonstration 0–100 number line or a line numbered 70 or 80–100, with pens
• demonstration unnumbered line with 20 or more intervals (*Number line 10*)
• OHP and OHT made from *Resource sheet A* (optional)

for each pair:
• paper and pens

Working with the children

Display a line numbered from 0 to 100 (or a line starting at, say, 80 and going up to 100) and attach to it an unnumbered line with 20 or more intervals.

Explain that you want the children to help you continue the line, writing in the numbers past 100. Help the children count out loud from, say, 80 to 100 and past 100, pointing out that the sequence after 100 is just like the sequence that starts at 0, except that each number has 'a hundred and' in front of it.

When we start at zero the numbers go zero, one, two, three, four, ... When we start at 100 the numbers go a hundred, a hundred and one, a hundred and two, a hundred and three, a hundred and four, ...

Now involve the children in writing in the numbers on the unnumbered segment of line. When the line is complete, count along it with the children, then rub out the numbers you have written in, except the 120. Repeat the above but counting backwards from 120.

Children working independently

In pairs, children now draw their own line from 90 to 120 on a blank piece of paper. As well as thinking about the sequence of numbers, they need to consider the spacing between the markers.

TEACHING POINT

●

The numbers after 100 follow a sequence similar to the sequence that starts at 0.

What comes after 99? ... And after 100? ...

How do you write that?

What number comes after 110?

Have you got room to write in the numbers as far as 120?

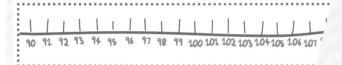

Gathering the children together

Display a number line from *Resource sheet A* on the OHP or draw a similar example on the board. Ask the children to help you fill in the missing numbers. Do the same with other lines from the sheet as appropriate.

Variations

◆ Introduce the activity on a counting stick, numbering it from 95 to 105.

◆ Together, make an odd/even line from 80 to 120, or 100 to 150, by writing odd numbers in red and even ones in blue. Talk about how to tell whether numbers above 100 are odd or even.

Simplifications

◆ Give children a pre-numbered line to copy.

◆ Provide an unnumbered line with markers to save them trying to fit the numbers into the available space on their paper.

◆ Work with numbers 90 to 110 and provide number cards to put in order, as a reminder.

93

106

98

107

100

◆ Children can use a calculator to add 1 to 80, then keep adding 1 repeatedly. This demonstrates how the numbers 'grow' above 100: '80, 81, 82, ... 99, 100, 101, 102, 103, ...'

Challenges

◆ Provide one or more of the lines from *Resource sheet A* for children to complete.

◆ Children can make number lines on blank paper
— from 0 to 200, numbered in tens
— from 50 to 150, numbered in ones or fives
— from 100 to 200, numbered in ones or fives

4 Numbers and the number system

Fractions

Snake pits

Objectives

★ recognise unit fractions
★ compare familiar fractions

Children help the teacher construct a line numbered from 0 to 15 in whole and half numbers and play a game which involves adding $\frac{1}{2}$, 1 or $1\frac{1}{2}$. They then play the game in pairs.

The game uses a familiar activity, drawing jumps on a number line, to help children gain experience of fractional numbers in order. The element of prediction in the game encourages them to add the fractions mentally.

You need

- demonstration unnumbered line with 30 intervals, with pen
  or
- board and marker
- spinner showing 0, $\frac{1}{2}$, 1, $1\frac{1}{2}$
- counters

  for each pair:
- fraction number line made from *Resource sheet B*
- spinner showing 0, $\frac{1}{2}$, 1, $1\frac{1}{2}$
- counters
- pencils

Working with the children

Ask the children to watch as you write in the whole numbers from 0 to 15 on the demonstration line, writing them by alternate markers. (You could draw this line on the board.) Ask:

> *Is there a number between zero and 1? And between 1 and 2? You see I haven't written a number by all the markers. What should I write?*

Then invite them to help you write in all the half numbers between the whole numbers.

Ring any ten of the numbers (but not 0 or 15).

Demonstrate the game by playing it yourself, against the class.

Each player (in this case you and the class as a whole) has five counters and the object is to lose as few of them as possible by the end of the game. Explain that, in the game, the ringed numbers are snake pits, and if you land on one you lose a counter. Take turns to:
- spin the spinner twice, say the numbers, and write them on the board
- choose which of the two numbers to use for your move (first move starts at 0)
- draw a jump of that size forwards, one player above the line and one below

TEACHING POINT

Between every two next-door neighbours on the number line there is a half number.

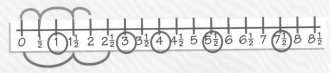

Continue taking turns like this, progressing towards 15. When you are near the end, you must wait until your spinner shows the exact number you need to reach 15. The winner is the player who loses fewer counters, not the person who gets to the end first.

> 0 $1\frac{1}{2}$
>
> I'll choose 0 because $1\frac{1}{2}$ puts me in the snake pit.

Children working independently

The children play the game in pairs on desktop fraction lines made from *Resource sheet B*.

Gathering the children together

You need the demonstration line marked up with fractions, and with numbers ringed, as before.

Ask the children to imagine you are on, say, 7. Spin the spinner and read out the number. Ask:

> *Would that jump forwards be safe, or would I land in a snake pit?*
>
> *What size of jump would not be safe?*

Ask several questions like this. Also ask them to imagine you are jumping back towards 0.

> *What jumps would be safe if you were going in the other direction?*
>
> *What size of jump would not be safe?*

Invite some children to demonstrate jumping backwards in jumps of $\frac{1}{2}$, 1 or $1\frac{1}{2}$. All the children say the numbers which are landed on.

Variations

◆ Children start at 15 and jump back towards 0, as in the last part of the main activity.

Challenges

◆ Children play on a line with 30 markers, labelled in quarters (that is, $0, \frac{1}{4}, \frac{1}{2}, \frac{3}{4}, 1, \ldots$). They use a spinner showing $0, \frac{1}{4}, \frac{1}{2}, \frac{3}{4}$ and 1.

◆ Children play on a line with 30 markers, labelled in thirds (that is, $0, \frac{1}{3}, \frac{2}{3}, 1, \ldots$). They use a spinner showing just $0, \frac{1}{3}, \frac{2}{3}, 1$, or one showing $0, \frac{1}{3}, \frac{2}{3}, 1, 1\frac{1}{3}$.

section 4

Making a fraction line

CLASS
then **PAIRS**

Objectives

★ begin to recognise simple fractions that are several parts of a whole, such as $\frac{3}{4}$
★ begin to recognise simple equivalent fractions
★ compare familiar fractions

You need

- demonstration unnumbered line with 30 intervals, with pen
or
- board and marker
- spinner showing $\frac{1}{4}$, $\frac{1}{2}$, $\frac{3}{4}$, 1
- counters

for each pair:
- desktop unnumbered line with 30 intervals (*Number line 9*), with pens

Often children learn that there are numbers less than 1 called 'a half' and 'a quarter' but do not understand that there are fractional numbers between *every* adjacent pair of whole numbers.

In order to help children learn this important idea, in this activity they make a line numbered in wholes, halves and quarters.

Working with the children

Use the demonstration line or draw a segment of number line on the board, with markers but no numbers.

Explain that this is part of a number line but that instead of just whole numbers it has whole numbers and the fractional numbers that come between them. Each interval is worth a quarter.

First, invite the children to help you write in the whole numbers; these will come every fourth marker. Doing this will alert you and the class if you go wrong later in the pattern of whole and fractional numbers.

Now, ask the children to help you write in the fractional numbers. When you get to $\frac{2}{4}$, simplify the fraction, or write both the unsimplified and simplified version.

After $\frac{1}{4}$ comes ... $\frac{2}{4}$, which is the same as $\frac{1}{2}$.
And now ... $\frac{3}{4}$ ... 1 ... And what comes after 1?

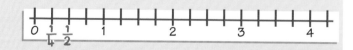

TEACHING POINT

A sequence of fractions follows a regular pattern, just as the whole numbers do.

Children working independently

Give each pair of children an unnumbered line with 30 intervals and ask them to number it in quarters from 0 to $7\frac{1}{2}$. Remind the children to fill in the whole numbers first.

Gathering the children together

Play 'Snake pits' (see p58) against the class using the line numbered in quarters, which will end on $7\frac{1}{2}$. Ring any ten of the numbers (but not 0 or $7\frac{1}{2}$).

You and the class each need five counters. Take turns to:
- spin the spinner (showing $\frac{1}{4}$, $\frac{1}{2}$, $\frac{3}{4}$, 1) twice, say the numbers, and write them on the board
- choose which of the two numbers to use for your move
- draw a jump of that size forwards from 0

Continue taking turns like this, progressing towards $7\frac{1}{2}$. If you land on a ringed number, you have fallen into a snake pit and you lose a counter.

When you are near the end, you must wait until your spinner shows the number you need to reach $7\frac{1}{2}$. The winner is the player who loses fewer counters, not the one who gets to the end first.

Variations

Simplification
◆ Children can first make a line numbered in halves, before progressing to quarters.

Challenges
◆ Children make a line numbered in quarters (or halves, thirds, sevenths, ninths, …) and their own spinner, then play 'Snake pits'.

◆ Children can make fraction lines starting at numbers other than 0, for example, between 5 and 10, or 10 and 20.

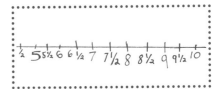

section 4

Fit the fractions in

CLASS
then **PAIRS**

Objectives

★ begin to position halves on a number line
★ compare familiar fractions
★ estimate length

This activity gives children lots of opportunities to position and use halves on a number line.

Each child has a card showing one of the whole or half numbers from 0 to 20; in turn they write in that number at the correct place on an empty line.

They then do a similar, but simpler, activity in pairs.

You need

• board and marker
• number cards showing whole and half numbers to 20 (made from *Resource sheets C–F*)

for each pair:
• long strip of paper (an A4 sheet cut in half or in quarters lengthwise and stuck end to end would do)
• 0–10 number cards
• pens

Working with the children

Draw a long line on the board and number one end 0 and the other 20.

Give out the cards, one to each child. There will probably be some left over, but make sure one child has the 10. First establish where 10 belongs.

> *Who has the card with 10 on it?.. Can you come and write 10 where it belongs on the line? ...*
> *That's right, it goes halfway between zero and 20.*

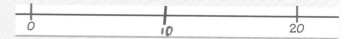

Check that the other children agree that the 10 is at the halfway point, then invite them to come one at a time and write in their number. You may want to start with numbers such as 5 and 15 in order to give the line some structure, before putting in the other numbers.

If necessary, some numbers may need to be rubbed out in order to make room for others.

> *Andy, there isn't room for your 2 because another number also has to go in there. What other number is that? ... 1½. We'll need to move the 2½ nearer to the 5. Where should the 2½ go? ...*
> *Halfway between 0 and 5. If I rub it out, can you write it in better spaced?*

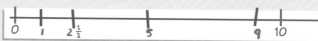

TEACHING POINT

On a number line a half lies midway between two whole numbers.

When all the children have written their numbers in, (assuming you have some cards left over) ask:

Are there some numbers missing? ... What do you think they are?

When a child suggests a missing number, ask them to come and find it in the pile and write it in.

Children working independently

Give each pair of children a set of cards with the whole numbers 0 to 10, and a long strip of paper. Ask them to draw a long line on their strips, and number the ends 0 and 10. They should shuffle the cards well, and put them in a pile face down.

They take turns to turn over a card, draw the marker and write the number in the correct place on the line. They should discuss and agree each position. When that is done, they add the half numbers in between.

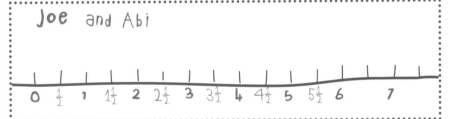

Gathering the children together

With the children, recite the sequence of numbers and half numbers from 0 to 20. The first time, children may look at the number lines they have made. Then recite the sequence again without any reference to the lines.

Variations

◆ Ask the children to close their eyes while you swap two of the numbers around. Can they say which two numbers have been moved?

◆ Children can use their wholes and halves line to play a racing game. They take turns to roll a dice showing: $\frac{1}{2}$, $\frac{1}{2}$, 1, $1\frac{1}{2}$, 2, $2\frac{1}{2}$ and move a counter that many steps along the line.

Simplifications

◆ This activity can be done on a counting stick, where the divisions are already marked. You need cards showing whole and half numbers from 0 to 5. Number the ends of the stick 0 and 5 and then discuss where to put the various number cards.

◆ Instead of writing whole and half numbers on the board, hang number cards on a washing line. This makes it easier to move the numbers and get equal spacing.

Challenge

◆ Children can make a quarters or thirds line.

section 5 Calculations

Addition and subtraction

Collecting conkers

Objectives

★ understand addition as steps
   along a number track
★ count on and back in ones from
   any small number
★ begin to understand that adding
   zero leaves a number unchanged

You need

for each pair or small group:
• desktop 1–10 number track, with
  'start' before the 1 (*Number line 2*)
• 'tree' and conkers (or just
  conkers) and play person (or
  similar tokens)
• dice or spinner showing 0, 1, 1,
  2, 2, 3

TEACHING POINT

●

**You can start at any
number and count on or
back.**

This is a game in which children move up and down a number track, collecting conkers one at a time from a 'tree' at the end of the track. It can be adapted to suit any topic of current interest: collecting pennies, lost ducklings …

The activity familiarises children with the mechanics of 'counting on' and 'counting back' on a number track or line, and helps them begin to learn the effect of starting on any number to 10 and moving on or back (that is, adding or subtracting) various numbers of steps.

Working with the children

Demonstrate the game to the whole class with two or more children playing collaboratively.

Put the 'tree' and pile of conkers at 10 on the number track, and the play person on Start. The children take turns to roll the dice and move the shared play person that many steps forwards.

start	1	2	3	4	5	6	7	8	9	10

Help the children count the steps; initially they may be confused that they are saying one set of numbers ("one, two") when actually moving their person along different numbers (such as 4, 5).

Encourage prediction.

> *The person is on 5 and you rolled a 2. If you start on 5 and add on 2, where do you think you will end up?*

When the play person reaches 10 it collects a conker and begins to bring it back to Start. Again, encourage prediction.

> *The person is on 9 and you rolled a 2. If you take two steps back towards the Start, where do you think you will end up?*

The game continues until all the conkers have been brought back, one by one, to the Start, although for this demonstration, the game need not be completed.

You will need to discuss with the class what to do if, for example, the person is on 9 and a 2 is thrown. Does it move to 10, collect the conker, and back to 9? Does it wait for a 1? Does it move to 10 and wait for the next dice-throw?

Children working independently

Children can play the same game in pairs or small groups. They could use the tree and conkers or invent their own 'scenario' and tokens. (You will need to decide how many conkers/tokens each group should have, depending on how long you want the game to last or how much practice you think the children need.) Each group can decide on their own rule for what happens when they get near 10 or Start.

Gathering the children together

Help the children practise their mental imagery by asking some simple questions about the number track when it is hidden from view.

> *Imagine our person is on 5 and she takes one step towards 10. Where will she end up?*

> *Now she takes two more steps forwards. Where does that take her to? ... How many more steps does she need to reach 10?*

Give some examples for moving backwards along the track so that children also have practice in mental subtraction.

◆ Sometimes children have problems keeping the play person and the conker together. You could play the game on a floor number track made from carpet tiles and using real children, with a basket, instead of play people.

◆ If you have children in your class who are familiar with a different number script, for example, Bengali or Urdu, provide a line numbered in that script for games like these.

Challenge

◆ Children can play this game on a track showing numbers to 12, 15 or 20, and a dice with slightly higher numbers.

◆ Children can play the game on a number line, such as the number ladder on *Number line 4*. They could collect 'apples' from a tree.

How many steps to 10?

Objectives

* ★ know by heart pairs of numbers with a total of 10
* ★ understand the operation of addition
* ★ begin to recognise that addition can be done in any order

You need

* floor 1–10 number track with 'start' before the 1
* 0–10 number cards with an extra 5 (divided into two sets: 0 to 5 and 5 to 10)
* board and marker
* demonstration number line to at least 10 (optional)

for each child:
* number fan (optional)

TEACHING POINT

There are several ways to reach 10 from 0 in two lots of steps.

A child takes a certain number of steps on a floor number track and stops. The group works out how many more steps are needed to reach 10. The activity is repeated with different numbers, giving the opportunity for using and practising number bonds to ten.

Note that this activity does not follow the usual session format.

Working with the children

Working with the floor track

The children sit beside the number track and one child stands on Start.

Invite a child to pick a card at random from the 5 to 10 set and ask them to show it to the group and read out the number. The child on the number track now takes that many steps forwards while the watchers count out loud. (You may need to show the children how to make each step with both feet. This means that when the child stops they will know what number they are on, which is not always the case if they use left and right feet alternately.)

Talk about the fact that the number on the track where the child is standing corresponds to the number on the card.

What number is Ravi on? ... And how many steps did he take?

Now ask the group how many steps they think the child will need to take in order to reach 10. Children can show their answer with number fans, or by holding up that number of fingers.

Choose one child to find the number card (from the 0 to 5 set) that represents the majority's guess and display it; ask the child on the number track to take the remaining steps to 10 while everybody counts the steps (not the numbers they step onto).

Discuss whether or not the majority guess was correct and, if not, ask a child to find the correct number card.

One child now holds up the two correct number cards while you record this pair of numbers on the board.

Continue with a different volunteer taking the steps, and different starting numbers. Record each pair of numbers.

steps to 10	
6	4
5	5
10	0

Reinforcing the learning

Finish the lesson by ordering the pairs of numbers on the board, with the help of the children. You could use a demonstration number line, to help children establish the order, and talk about what would happen with other starting numbers.

steps to 10	
5	5
6	4
7	3
8	2
9	1
10	0

Suppose Stacey took four steps to start with. Can you tell from the chart how many more she would need to make to reach 10?

Watch me while I make steps with my fingers on the number line ... From 4 you need another six steps, just like when Harry was on 6 he needed another four steps.

You can demonstrate the relationship between 'four steps and another six steps' and 'six steps and another four steps' with number cards.

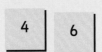

The cards are ordered differently, but in both cases the numbers add to 10.

section 5

Variations

◆ One child stands on Start and one on 10, facing each other. The first child walks forward, say, four steps to 4. The class then predict how many steps the second child must take from 10 to reach the same number.

◆ On a floor number track, a child takes some steps with the left foot first, then takes more steps with the right foot first. Explore pairs of left-steps and right-steps that take them from Start to 10.

◆ Use a number track on the magnetic board. 'Walk' a magnetic person along the track and ask the children to predict how many more steps the person must make in order to reach 10.

Challenge
◆ Explore all the pairs of steps that make 12, or 8, or 15, ...

Starting at 10 and 20

CLASS
then **PAIRS**

Objectives

★ add a single digit to 10 or 20
★ begin to partition a number into tens and ones
★ understand place value

You need

- demonstration 0–30 number line, with pen
- 0–9 number cards

  for each pair:
- desktop 0–30 number line (*Number line 5*)
- 0–9 number cards
- counters, play people or other tokens

TEACHING POINT

●

Look at the units digit to find out what has been added on to 10 or 20.

Children make steps in secret from 10 or 20, according to the number on a card. The other children see the end result and work out the number on the card.

This activity underlines the pattern within the decades: looking at the ones digit tells you how many steps you are from the last tens-number such as 10 or 20.

Working with the children

Draw a ring round 10 on the demonstration line. Give one child a number card but don't let anyone else know what number it is. Now tell the child to make that many steps from 10 along the line, using a finger. The final number should be ringed.

The rest of the children count the steps as they are made then hold up their fingers to show this number.

Ask the child making the steps to show everybody the card. Talk about the fact that when you start at 10 and take, say, three steps you end on 13.

13 starts with a 1 just like 10 does. And it ends with a 3, because it is three steps on from 10.

After one or two goes like this, tell the children who are watching to close their eyes so they can't count the steps as they are made.

Now, open your eyes. Can you work out how many steps Satinder made? ... How do you know? ... Because he ended up on 17 which means he moved seven steps on from 10.

When the children are used to the activity, start steps at 20.

Can you work out how many steps Rachel took? ... How do you know? ... She ended up on 25 which means she moved five steps on from 20. 25 starts with a 2 just like 20 does. 25 means 20 and 5 more. It ends with a 5, because it is five steps on from 20.

Children working independently

The children can do this in pairs using counters or play people on a desktop 0–30 number line. Child A chooses where to start (0, 10 or 20) and places the token on that number. They then pick a card from the 0–9 pack and move the token that number of steps, while Child B looks away, or closes their eyes.

When Child A has made the steps, Child B looks at where the token is and has to say how many steps were taken. The children then look at the number card together to see if Child B was correct.

The children swap roles and repeat the activity.

Gathering the children together

Help the children practise their mental imagery by asking some questions based on this activity but without making steps on any line.

> *Imagine Simon is on 10 and he takes five steps forwards. Where will he end up? ... How do you know that?*

> *Suppose Tracey is on 20 and takes five steps forwards. Where will she end up? ... How do you know that?*

> *Suppose Shubi started on 10 and is now on 16. How many steps did she take? ... How do you know?*

Variations

◆ Children use a 0–100 line and take steps from any of the tens-numbers. Although the numbers are larger, the game is no harder as the principle is the same.

Simplifications

◆ Child A picks two number cards, puts them face up on the table, then takes steps from 10 for one of the cards. Child B must work out which was chosen. For the child guessing, this makes the task easier.

◆ Model the process of adding a single digit to 10 or 20 using place value cards.

Challenge

◆ Instead of starting at 10, children start at 9 (or 11). This is an introduction to the technique of adding 9 and 11 by adding 10 and adjusting.

Stations

Objectives

★ mentally subtract a single digit from a 'teens' number, crossing the tens

★ understand subtraction as steps back along a number line

You need

• OHP and OHT made from *Resource sheet G*, with pen
• 1–6 dice
• a matchstick, cube or paper clip (to represent the train)
• board and marker
• demonstration 0–20 number line (optional)

TEACHING POINT

●

You can work out where you will end up by counting the steps on your mental number line.

Children choose certain numbers on the 0–20 line to be 'stations'. They then predict whether or not a 'train' moving back a certain number of intervals will stop at a station.

This activity uses a different shape of number line, encouraging children to think flexibly about numbers in order. They also have to calculate mentally.

Note that this activity does not follow the usual lesson format.

Playing the game

Put the OHT on the overhead projector and ring the 20. Tell the children that a train is going to travel from the 20 back to the terminus at 0; it will stop on the way, preferably at stations but also between stations.

Ask six children each to choose a number between 0 and 20 (not 0 or 20) to be the stations.

Ring these numbers on the OHT, and write them on the board.

Put the 'train' on 20, roll the dice, and say the number. Move the train that number of steps back towards 0, while the children count the steps.

If you land on a station, everybody cheers; if not, they boo: well-run trains only stop at stations. (If cheering and booing are not appropriate, try thumbs up or down. If children hold their thumbs close to their faces, this has the advantage that their responses are more private; they are less likely to copy

Our stations today
are at
3 5 8 9 10 15

each other and it is easier for you to assess individual children.)

Continue like this until you are near 0. You must roll the correct number to reach the terminus.

When the children are familiar with the game, cover up the OHT before rolling the dice. Say what the dice-number is and ask children to look at the station numbers written on the board and predict whether or not the train will stop at a station. Uncover the OHT and check their predictions.

Reinforcing the learning

Talk with the children about how they work out where a train will stop.

> *If the train is on 13 and the dice says 4, where will the train end up? ... How do you know that?*

Pick up on, and encourage, any short cuts the children describe.

> *Does anyone else do that? ... Let's look at that method on a number line.*

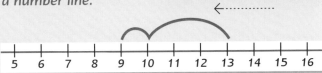

I did it in two jumps. I went back three to 10, and then another one to 9

$$\leftarrow\text{-----------}$$

| | | | | | | | | | | | |
|5|6|7|8|9|10|11|12|13|14|15|16|

> *Sharon, you said that if the train goes back five steps from 10 it reaches 5, because 5 and 5 makes 10. Can you show us what you mean on the number line?*

Variations

◆ Move the train forwards from 0 to 20 for practising mental addition.

◆ Divide the class into two teams and give each a different shaped 'train' to move on the OHT. The teams take it in turns to roll a dice (or do it for them). Whichever team stops at most stations wins the game.

◆ Make a giant railway track number line so a group of children can play the game with a teaching assistant. When the adult rolls the dice, the children must close their eyes while they make their predictions.

Challenge
◆ Roll two dice and invite children to choose one of the numbers – if possible, one which will take the train to a station.

PAIRS

Objectives

★ partition a number into tens and ones
★ understand the operation of subtraction
★ count back in tens and ones

You need

for each pair:
- desktop line with 100 intervals numbered in fives (*Number line 7*)
- felt-tipped pens in two colours
- 1–20 dice

Children roll a 1–20 dice and predict where they will land if they take that number of steps back from 100 towards 0. They then take the steps, breaking the number down if appropriate into ten and some ones to make the calculation easier. Because the line is numbered only in fives, the structure of the number system is clear, which can support the children in their mental calculation. Note that this activity does not follow the usual lesson format.

Children working independently

Spend a few minutes with the children practising counting backwards from various numbers between 0 and 100, in tens and ones. Then explain the game.

Both players start at 100. When it is their turn they:
- roll the dice and say the number
- predict where they will end up if they take that many steps back towards 0, saying the number out loud (without touching the number line)
- make that many steps backwards with their finger, and write in the number where they end up
- write their initial by that number if their prediction was correct; if not, they take five steps forward, towards 100, and put their initial by that number instead

> I've rolled 11, I think I'll land on the 85.

> No I was wrong. It's 89. I must go five steps to 94.

It is important that the partners pay attention to each other's predictions and call each other on any cheating, whether intentional or unintentional.

The first person to reach a number below 10 is the winner.

TEACHING POINT

A number can be partitioned to make it easier to subtract it.

As they are playing, encourage children to break numbers larger than 10 into a ten-jump and a smaller number. Help them to see that they can use their understanding of place value to subtract 10, and then adjust the answer.

> *Kayleigh, you are now on 94 and you need to go back thirteen spaces. Where will a ten-jump take you back to? What is 10 less than 94? ... So what is 13 less?*

Reinforcing the learning

Work with just a single pair, or with all the pairs who have been playing. Help the children practise their mental imagery by asking some questions based on this activity, without reference to the number line.

> *Imagine Aaron is on 90 and he takes three steps back. Where will he end up? ... How did you know that?*

> *Suppose Mahua is on 73 and she takes fifteen steps back. How are you going to work out where she ends up? Suppose she goes back ten first, where will she reach? ... And how much further has she still got to go?*

Variations

◆ Children can play the game racing forwards. They start at 0 and race towards 100. The first person to pass 90 wins.

◆ Children ring ten numbers at random then play the game. If a player lands on a ringed number they jump back an extra 10, but only if they can predict correctly where the jump will take them to.

Simplification

◆ Children start at 50 and use a 0–9 dice.

Challenges

◆ Children use a 1–6 or 0–9 dice and double the number they roll.

◆ Children use two 1–6 or 0–9 dice. Can they predict where they will land after moving back for both dice?

◆ Children use a 0–1000 line, numbered in tens, and a dice showing 50, 60, 70, 80, 90, 100, to play either 'Race back' or 'Race forwards'.

◆ Children use a line numbered in fractions.

section
5

Calculating with two-digit numbers

CLASS
then **INDIVIDUALS**

Objectives

★ recognise that addition can be done in any order but subtraction can't
★ develop the mental addition and subtraction strategy of 'partition and recombine'

You need

• board and marker
• demonstration line with 100 intervals numbered in fives, with pen

for each child:
• desktop line with 100 intervals numbered in fives (*Number line 7*)
• felt-tipped pens

As a development of the previous activity, children use a number line to help in calculating with two-digit numbers; they break one number into tens and ones and deal with these separately.

Having a line with only every fifth marker numbered encourages children to use their knowledge of the number system rather than relying on a ready-made display of numbers.

Working with the children

Addition by partitioning and recombining

> 25 + 38
> 38 + 25

Write a two-digit addition sum on the board. Remind children that, when adding, it is easier if you start with the larger number. If appropriate, rearrange the sum.

Explain that you are going to demonstrate how to make 'adding on' big numbers easy by doing them a bit at a time. Write in the first number where it belongs on the line.

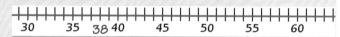

Say that rather than draw lots of single steps, you will make jumps of ten, and then a few steps. Invite the children to help you break down the second number and write it on the board.

> 38 + 25 =
> 38 + 10 + 10 + 5 =

Then draw the jumps of ten, writing in the numbers you pause on. Finally, deal with the ones digit. If this involves crossing the tens, draw two small jumps, pausing on the ten-number as you go.

Instead of the last five steps I'm going to do a jump of two, to take me to the tens number, and then another of three. That makes five.

So we started at 38 and went 48 ... 58 ... 60 ... 63.

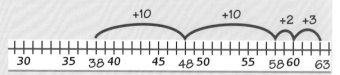

TEACHING POINT

●

When adding or subtracting two-digit numbers, do jumps of ten or more rather than single steps.

Write the size of each jump above the line as a reminder to the children.

Finally, complete the sum on the board.

> 38 + 25 =
> 38 + 10 + 10 + 5 = 63

Tell children that an even quicker way is to add the 20 in one big jump, then add the ones. Demonstrate this – but don't expect all children to use this method straight away.

Subtraction

Subtractions can be done in just the same way, splitting the second number into tens and ones. Once children are familiar with this work they may be able to suggest further short cuts.

> *The problem is 43 minus 24. How might I do that? Where should I start? ... Jump back twenty and then do a jump of three and a single step?*

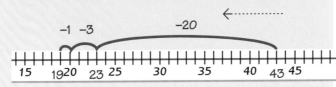

Encourage children also to consider the method of counting on for subtraction: starting at 24 and jumping on in tens and ones to 43, then totalling the distance jumped.

Children working independently

When you are confident that the children understand the process, give them a few addition and subtraction problems to solve on their own using desktop lines.

Gathering the children together

Discuss children's methods with them. If they suggest different, or quicker, ways of breaking the second number down, encourage these: whatever method works for the child is acceptable. For example, children may add a number such as 45 by adding 20 and 20, then adding 5. Or they may subtract a number such as 39 by subtracting 40 and going forward a step. Or, in the subtraction example above they might do '43 take away 23 is 20, and take away another 1 is 19'.

section 5

Variations

Simplifications

◆ Practise jumping in tens orally, from 0 and from other numbers, both backwards and forwards.

◆ Stick to numbers with totals below 50, and where no crossing of tens is involved.

◆ Do a calculation such as 24 + 14 on a numbered line first before doing it on a 'fives-and-tens-only' line.

◆ When drawing a jump of ten, remind children, if necessary, how to draw ten single steps and then turn this into a jump.

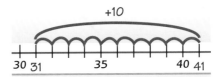

Challenge

◆ Give children a 50–150 line numbered in fives, and set problems within that range.

> 93 + 47
> 119 – 67

Objectives

★ recognise that addition can be done in any order
★ understand addition as steps forward along a number line
★ develop the mental addition strategy of 'partition and recombine'

You need

• demonstration 0–30 number line, with pen
• board and marker

for each child:
• paper and pen/pencil
• number fan (optional)

This activity and the next one, which both dispense with a physical number line altogether, build on the previous activity which used a line with only every fifth marker numbered.

These activities help children to develop and use their mental imagery when adding and subtracting.

The activity on this page deals with adding single digits (subtraction is included under 'Variations'); the next one involves adding and subtracting larger numbers.

Working with the children

Working with a number line

Ask the children some questions using small numbers which involve crossing ten, and say you want them to work out the answers in their heads.

What is 7, and 5 more? ... What is 9 add 6? ...

Talk with the children about how they do the problems in their heads, and acknowledge all methods. Say that you want to teach everybody to use an 'empty number line' for problems that are just too hard to do in their heads.

Start with the 0–30 line and talk about ways of adding small numbers on a number line. For example, a child might suggest that one way to add 7 and 5 is to start at 7 and draw five steps.

Explain that if you know all the number pairs that make 10, there are quicker ways. If no one suggests them, demonstrate the following two, writing the result on the board:

$$7 + 5 =$$
$$7 + 3 + 2 = 12$$

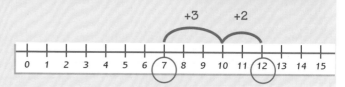

We can start at 7 and make it up to 10 in one jump of three, because we know that 7 and 3 is 10. Then we work out how much is left (that is, 2), and do it in another jump.

TEACHING POINT

●

When adding or subtracting small numbers you can do it in two bits, pausing on the ten-number as you go.

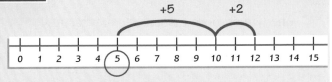

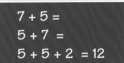

$7 + 5 =$
$5 + 7 =$
$5 + 5 + 2 = 12$

Or we can start with the 5 and make a jump of five, because we know 5 and 5 makes 10, then deal with the 2 remaining.

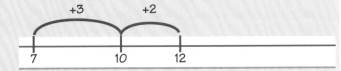

+5   +2

0 1 2 3 4 5 6 7 8 9 10 11 12 13 14 15

Working with an empty line

Now move on to adding small numbers on an imaginary number line, using the same problem that you did on the numbered line. Draw a simple line and put the starting number at one end.

Explain that you are doing this addition just the same way as on the numbered line, in two jumps. But this line has no numbers on; instead, you can write in the numbers you need.

I start at 7 and make it up to 10 (jump of three) then I work out how much is left and do that (jump of two).

+3   +2

7   10   12

Ask a child to demonstrate the other way: 5 + 5 + 2. Do one or two more problems like this, adding a small number to a number below twenty. Involve the children as much as possible.

Children working independently

Write up similar addition problems on the board and ask the children to try and work them out however they like, drawing empty number lines if they choose. They should write down the answers.

Gathering the children together

Ask children to tell you the answers or display them with their number fans if they have them.

Talk briefly with the children about the mental methods they used, then invite less confident children to help you check each answer by drawing two jumps on an empty number line.

Variations

◆ Children can roll a 0–9, 1–12 or 1–20 dice to generate numbers to add or subtract.

Other methods

◆ It is important to acknowledge that there are many methods for adding small numbers. For example, if asked to add 8 and 6 some children may want to start at 8 and jump on 2 then 4. Others may prefer to double 6 and add on 2. Or add 10 and 6 and take away 2. Demonstrate on the line methods suggested by the children, and discuss with them which they prefer.

Subtraction

◆ On a future occasion show children how subtracting small numbers can also be done using two jumps. Use calculations which involve crossing the 10.

Challenge

◆ Ask children to use the empty line method line to solve problems such as:

7 + 5
17 + 5
27 + 5
37 + 5

Discuss the pattern in the answers.

section 5

Adding and subtracting

CLASS
then **INDIVIDUALS**

Objectives

★ recognise that addition can be done in any order
★ add or subtract a pair of numbers bridging through a multiple of 10 and adjusting

You need

• board and marker

for each child:
• paper and pen/pencil

This activity builds on the previous one, using the empty line as a tool when dealing with addition and subtraction. Instead of adding a single digit, crossing 10, the problems involve two-digit numbers and larger jumps.

The activity involves work at a fairly simple level, but the principles of using the line are the same whatever the complexity of the calculation: children write or draw just as many numbers as they need to keep track of their workings.

Working with the children

Addition of two-digit numbers

Write on the board a problem involving the addition or subtraction of two two-digit numbers.

> *I want to do 32 + 57. Which number shall I start with?*
> *... The 57, because it's larger.*

32 + 57
57 + 32

Draw a simple line, put the starting number, 57, at one end and remind children about the empty line.

> *I am going to do this addition by breaking it into bits. The number line has no numbers on; I will write in the numbers I need.*

Invite ideas as to how to tackle the problem, and acknowledge all suggestions. Choose one to demonstrate on the line (starting at 57 and jumping on 32 is one method but not the only one). Draw the jumps and steps and write in the numbers after each, for example:

> *I start at the larger number, 57. Then do a jump of ten to ... 67. And another, and another ... And finally a jump of two. The final number is ...*

```
      +10        +10        +10      +2
   ⌒          ⌒          ⌒      ⌒
  57         67         77      87 89
```

Encourage children to consider the method of adding the tens in one big jump, then adding the ones. Demonstrate this – but don't expect all the children to use the method straight away.

TEACHING POINT

●

When adding or subtracting two- and three-digit numbers you can draw just as much of a number line as you need.

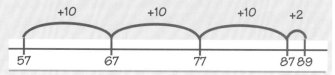

Subtraction

Ask one of the children to come to the board and suggest a subtraction calculation with two-digit numbers. Support the child in finding their own way to solve this problem using an empty number line.

52 – 27

What number will you start with? ... 52. And where will you put it? ... At the right-hand end of the line, because it is larger than the number you are going to subtract. So which method do you want to choose? ... Jumping back 30 and then forwards 3?

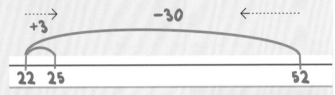

If necessary, help the child draw the jumps and write in the numbers, then ask them to write a number sentence on the board, showing the stages they did it in.

52 – 27
52 – 30 + 3 = 25

Encourage children to consider other methods for doing the same subtraction, for example, starting at the lower number and jumping on in tens and ones to the higher, then totalling the distance jumped.

If appropriate, work through one or two more problems together before the children move on to work alone.

Children working independently

Ask children to invent their own problems to solve on an empty number line. At this stage it is more important that they become confident with the method than that they choose calculations which will challenge them, but they should use two-digit numbers.

Gathering the children together

Invite one or two children to demonstrate their problems and solutions on the board. Discuss their methods and ask the other children to suggest other ways of solving them. Accept all methods which work – whatever helps an individual child is acceptable. However, it is important they see a range of methods so that they can widen their own available strategies.

Variations

◆ Give children a pack of number cards with which to generate problems. They can either deal themselves four single-digit cards, and arrange them to make two numbers, or deal two 0–100 cards.

3 2 + 7 1

1 4 7 – 9

18 + 47

Simplification

◆ Children can solve some problems where a single digit is added to or taken away from a two-digit number to give them confidence, before moving on to work with two two-digit numbers.

Challenge

◆ It is important that at some point children have experience of problems where they cross 100. For example, when subtracting 15 from 103 children can start at 103, jump back 10, then 3, then 2, to reach 88.

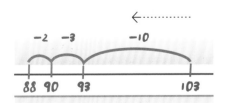

section 6 Calculations

Multiplication and division

Bears in pairs

Objectives

★ use and understand the vocabulary of doubling and of multiplication
★ understand multiplication as repeated addition
★ count on in twos

You need

• carpet tiles numbered 1 to 10
• 1–10 number cards
• 20 bears/dolls/soft toys
• board and marker

for each pair:
• desktop 1–10 number track (*Number line 1*)
• 1–10 number cards
• 20 tokens (cubes/miniature teddies/cars, shells …)
• paper and pens/pencils

Children put two bears (or other objects) on each number of the track and count them in twos.

This kind of activity gives children practical experience of multiplying by two and can help them make links with more formal experience of multiplication and the tables.

Working with the children

Give a number tile to each of ten children and invite them to lay them down on the floor one at a time, to make a number track from 1 to 10. Ask the children to sit beside this number track.

Pick a number card and display it. Ask the children to help you put out one bear on each tile from 1 to that number.

Count the bears, establish how many there are, and write the number on the board.

Now invite the children to help you put out one more bear on each tile.

Count the bears one at a time, establish how many there are, and write the number on the board.

Practise counting the bears in twos, perhaps by saying each number but whispering the odd numbers and emphasising the even ones.

*One, **two**, three, **four**, five, **six**, …*

TEACHING POINT

Counting in twos from 0 gives the pattern of the ×2 table.

Remove all the bears from the track. Pick other number cards and each time invite children to put two bears on each tile. Each time count the bears in twos and record the numbers.

> *The card says 2 so we put two bears on each tile up to 2.*

> *Count with me: two, four bears.*

Children working independently

Working with desktop number tracks, children repeat the activity in pairs. They pick a card and identify that number on the track, then put two tokens on each square up to that number. They count the tokens in twos, and record both the numbers on a piece of paper, as you did on the board.

Gathering the children together

Display one of the children's records and talk about the numbers. (Copy the numbers onto the board if necessary for all the children to see.)

> *Each of these numbers is twice as big as the one before it.*

> *If you double the number on the left you get its partner number on the right.*

Then display a different record. Hide numbers in turn and ask the children to tell you what each one is, and how they know.

> *The left-hand number is a 5. What is the right-hand number?*

> *Over here on the right is 6. What is the number on the left?*

section
6

Variations

◆ Instead of putting two bears on each tile, use the children themselves.

◆ Another way for children to generate the 'pattern of twos' is to make a number track in two colours: say, the odd numbers in red and the even ones in yellow. As they say the names of the yellow numbers they effectively count in twos: 2, 4, 6, 8, …

◆ Children use an ordinary number track and put one bear on each number: a blue bear on every odd number and an orange bear on every even one.

Challenge

◆ Help children combine their records from the main activity and order the pairs of numbers on the board. Use the multiplication symbols to convert this joint record into the two times table.

CLASS
then **PAIRS**

Objectives

★ understand multiplication as repeated addition
★ know by heart multiplication facts for the 2, 3 and 5 times tables
★ recognise two-digit multiples of 2, 5 or 10

Children make or draw equal jumps to reach a target number below 100; they record what sizes of jumps do and don't 'work'.

The links that this activity has with other experiences should be made explicit to the children, especially:
● dividing collections of objects into equal-sized sets
● work on multiples using calculators
● the times tables

You need

• demonstration 0–100 number line, with pen
• board and marker
• calculator or OHP calculator and OHP

for each pair:
• desktop 0–100 number line (*Number line 6*)
• paper and pencils

Working with the children

Ask a child to choose a target number between 20 and 30 and ring that number on the demonstration line.

Tell the children you are going to draw jumps of two from 0. Ask them whether they think you will land on the number chosen.

The children can make predictions by putting their thumbs up for 'yes' and down for 'no' (or privately by writing the answer in their rough book). Then draw the jumps while the children say with you the numbers you are landing on.

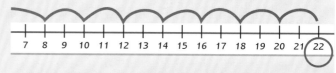

... 8, 10, 12, 14, 16, 18, 20, 22. Yes, I did land on 22.

Children working independently

Now write up some target numbers on the board (choose numbers which are divisible by 2, 3 or 5). Ask the children to work in pairs and choose one of these target numbers to ring on their desktop line. (Children should choose numbers to suit them. Some will stick to the lower numbers; others can work with the higher numbers.) They choose a jump size – twos, threes or fives. They should then investigate whether they can reach their target from 0 in jumps of that size.

TEACHING POINT

Some numbers you can get to in equal jumps and some you can't.

They then investigate what other sizes of jump do and don't work for their target number.

Encourage the children to predict which numbers will and won't work.

Do you think jumps of three will work? ... Why?

Encourage the children to make deductions from what they already know.

Do you think jumps of four will work?

What nearby numbers do you know you can reach in jumps of four?

Children could record their work in two lists – those sizes of jump that do and those that don't reach their target.

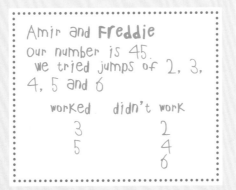

Amir and **Freddie**
Our number is 45.
We tried jumps of 2, 3, 4, 5 and 6

worked	didn't work
3	2
5	4
	6

Gathering the children together

Display one of the children's recordings and talk about what they found out.

Demonstrate with a calculator how to check the results using division.

Another way to see if 45 can be reached in jumps of three is to divide 45 by 3 on the calculator. I press '45 ÷ 3 =' and I get 15. That means that 15 jumps of three take me to 45.
Now, what would I press to check whether 45 can be reached in jumps of four?

Variations

◆ Make jumps of two from 0 on a 0–100 line to identify all the even numbers; jumps of two from 1 will identify all the odd numbers.

◆ Choose a times table that children are learning, say, the 5 times table. Children take turns to pick a number card from a pack of 0–100 cards and predict whether they can get to that number in equal jumps of five, then test it out on a number line. If right, they score a point.

Simplification
◆ Children who have difficulties with the physical act of drawing equal-sized jumps might find it helpful to use a 'jumper' of the appropriate size; this is a wooden or cardboard stick the same length as the jump-size they are working with. They can put it in position and it will show them where to start and finish the next jump.

Equal jumps

CLASS
then **INDIVIDUALS**

Objectives

★ understand multiplication as repeated addition
★ know by heart multiplication facts for the 2, 3, 4, 5 and 10 times tables

You need

- counting stick
- number labels (Post-it notes would do)
- demonstration 0–100 number line, with pen
- calculator or OHP calculator and OHP

  for each child:
- *Resource sheet H*
- pen/pencil

TEACHING POINT

If you make equal jumps from 0 you get the number pattern of the multiplication tables.

Children count with you in equal jumps from 0, using a counting stick. They then work alone, writing the numbers in on an unnumbered line. The line provides markers that are equally spaced, and where the spaces can be designated as having any value – at this stage, 2, 3, 4, 5 or 10. It is important to place the activity in context for children, for example, by making links with similar work on a numbered line and with a calculator, as well as with 'real life' occasions where it is helpful to count in equal jumps.

Working with the children

Spend a minute or two counting in twos, fives or tens to 20 (or 50 or 100) and back again.

Put labels 0 and 10 at either end of the counting stick.
> *This line goes from 0 to 10. What would halfway be? ... How do you know?*

Point to the other markers and establish what these numbers are. Each time, stick the appropriate number label on at the right place on the stick.

Now remove the labels, leaving the 0 and replacing the 10 label with a 20.
> *This time the line goes from 0 to 20. What would halfway be this time? ... How do you know?*

Point to the other markers and establish what these numbers are. Each time, discuss how children know this, then stick the appropriate number label on the stick.

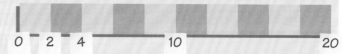

Finally, remove the labels, except for 0.

This time the intervals on the line are all worth 5. What will the final number be? ... What number belongs here, on the first marker after the zero? ... How do you know?

Children working independently

Give children one or more blank lines from *Resource sheet H* to fill in, in the same way that you have been numbering the markers on the counting stick. You can present the work in various ways:

- fill in 0 and the final number yourself, and ask children to number the other markers
- fill in 0 yourself, and tell children what size of interval to use; they number the other markers
- present the blank lines as they are and ask children to choose a final number, or size of interval, from a selection you write on the board, then number all the markers

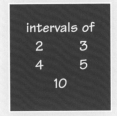

final number	
20	30
40	50
100	

intervals of	
2	3
4	5
10	

Gathering the children together

Display one or more of the children's filled-in lines and talk about the pattern of the numbers. Make links between counting in equal jumps and the numbers in the multiplication tables.

Show the children how to check the numbers they have filled in by drawing equal-sized jumps on a numbered line.

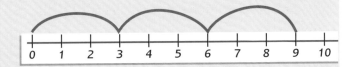

Finally, demonstrate how to do the same thing on a calculator, by adding the same number repeatedly (using the constant function if you so choose).

Variations

◆ Children can make jumps of any size from 0 (or another number) on a numbered line. Can they predict what numbers they will land on? What number patterns do they notice?

◆ Children jump back from 100 in equal-sized jumps. Again, can they predict what numbers they will land on? What number patterns do they notice?

Challenge

◆ Label the first marker 1, 2, 4 or 7. Challenge children to make jumps of two, three, four, five or ten and label the other markers appropriately.

Real world problems

◆ Use the number line or calculator to model equal jumps (both multiplication and division) whenever an occasion arises: seven children each need two sheets of paper; three notice boards each hold eight A4 sheets; how many tables are needed to seat 32 children with six children to a table ...

section 6

Multiplying in the real world

Objectives

★ understand multiplication as repeated addition
★ solve problems involving numbers in 'real life'

You need

• board and marker
• prepared word problems

for each child:
• paper and pens/pencils

It is important that children use the number line to deal with real-world numbers, not just abstract numbers.

Here children are shown how to use the empty number line for multiplying by repeated addition in a real-life context.

The main activity involves work on the 4 times table, which children at this stage are probably learning but have not mastered; it can, of course, be used with higher numbers.

Working with the children

Ideally this activity should be introduced with a genuine situation requiring a multiplication calculation; however, not many such 'real' problems occur in the classroom, so you may need to invent a hypothetical one. The example here is based on children needing dice for a number game. There are six tables and each table needs four dice; before fetching them from the stock room, you need to know how many will be needed.

> 6 tables each need 4 dice. How many must we fetch?

> 6 x 4 =

Write the problem on the board. Check with the children that they know what kind of problem it is.

> *What operation would you use to find out how many dice we need if each table is to have four? ... You could use addition; keep adding four ...*

> *Or you could use multiplication. You could work out what six lots of four are.*

Discuss how they might work out the answer.

> *You could count out cubes and pretend they were dice. But I want you to learn how to do problems like this more quickly than by counting. I am going to show you how you could do it by drawing your own really simple number line.*

> *It is a method called repeated addition – it is like adding and also like multiplying, both at once.*

Draw a line, put 0 at one end and explain what you are doing.

I am going to do this on a number line with no numbers. I will just write in the numbers I need.

Draw the jumps of four and get the children to count with you in fours, and help you write in the numbers after each jump.

One table needs four dice, two tables need ... eight dice, and three tables ... twelve dice ...

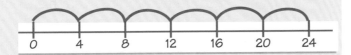

Six tables need ... 24 dice. So I would need to fetch 24 dice.

Complete the calculation on the board, read it aloud and interpret it with the children.

6 x 4 = 24

Children working independently

Provide some more word problems and ask children to write down the calculation. (Try to use problems at a level just beyond children's knowledge of multiplication facts – there is no point in them drawing number lines if they know the answers or can quickly work them out in their heads.) If they do already know the answer, they should simply write that down. If not, they work out the answer by drawing jumps on an empty number line, then complete the written calculation.

Each model car needs 4 wheels. How many wheels will 9 cars need?

How many straight lines are there in 5 triangles?

Gathering the children together

Go over one or two of the word problems with the children, then spend a few minutes helping them invent their own repeated addition problems. Record these for use on another occasion.

Variations

◆ Give pairs of children two 0–9 dice with which to generate their own repeated additions.

Simplification

◆ Repeated addition on an empty line depends on children being able to count in twos, threes, fours and so on, even if they cannot recite their multiplication tables. Children who have difficulty with this work may well need to practise counting from 0 in groups of various sizes.

Challenge

◆ Introduce problems involving multiplying a single-digit number by a number between 10 and 20. Children will need to adapt the method of repeated addition suggested here. For example, to do 3×12 a child might choose to split the jumps of twelve into jumps of ten and two.

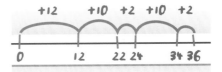

section 6

section 7 Solving problems

'Real life' problems

Grocery sale

Objectives

★ solve word problems involving money
★ explain how the problem was solved

Knowing how to add, subtract, multiply and divide is meaningless unless children can apply these operations appropriately.

This activity uses a simple and familiar situation, price

reductions in a food shop, to give children practice in using a number line or empty line to solve a subtraction problem.

You need

• demonstration 0–100 number line, with pen
• board and marker

for each child or pair:
• money arrow cards (optional)
• *Resource sheet I*
• desktop 0–100 number line (*Number line 6*)(optional)
• paper and pen/pencil

Working with the children

Set up a context with the children, involving a supermarket or corner shop where certain items are being offered with 15p off. Ask the children to suggest items for the sale which might cost between, say, 70p and £1.40 and their (pre-offer) prices.

cola 92p
biscuits 80p
grapes £1.37
spaghetti rings 78p

Choose a problem where the starting price is less than £1 and ask the children to try to work out its reduced price mentally. (You could ask any children who succeed at this to display their answers with money arrow cards; this would allow you to see who has got the right answer without giving the game away to those who haven't yet worked it out.)

Using a numbered line

Now demonstrate how to use a numbered 0–100 line to do the subtraction involved. For children who have not yet worked out the answer, this is a useful method to use; other children can use it to check their mental calculation.

The cola costs 92p. Jump back ten to 82, then another five to ... 77. What is 15p less than 92p? ... 77p. The cheap offer price for the cola is 77p.

TEACHING POINT

To subtract 15, go back 10 then another 5.

Using an empty line

Now demonstrate how to do the same calculation with an empty line.

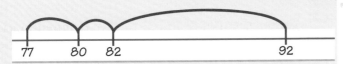

I start at 92p. That is the price of the cola before 15p is taken off. Then I go back ten to ... 82.

Then I go back five more in two stages. First I take off two to reach 80. Then how much is left to take off? ... Three more. 80 go back three takes me to 77. So 92p take off 15p leaves 77p.

Demonstrate a similar problem involving a starting price that is more than £1.

Children working independently

Give pairs of children (or individuals) a copy of *Resource sheet I*. Decide for each pair how many calculations they should do and ask them to choose that many items to 'buy'. For each one they must work out its sale price. Some children will be able to do this straight away using the empty number line method; they should do any workings on paper and write the answer on the problem sheet. Others will need a numbered line, at least to start with, but should be encouraged to try using an empty line.

Gathering the children together

Ask one or two children to choose an item each and demonstrate their method for solving the subtraction problem.

Encourage children to internalise the empty number line method by naming a new starting price and helping them to subtract 15p mentally.

There is a tin of soup at 76p. To find the new price, take off 10p. What is 10 less than 76? ... 66.

Now to take off 5 from 66 is easy. 6 take away 5 is ... 1; so 66 take away 5 is 61.

The new price of the soup is 61p.

Variations

◆ Have a sale in the class shop and reduce everything by 10p, 9p, 5p or 3p.

◆ Help children write a number sentence for each calculation and interpret the answer.

> butter
> 89 – 15 = 74
> sale price is 74p

Simplification

◆ Direct children to choose items below £1, or provide a sheet with even lower prices. Ask children to reduce prices by 5p or 10p.

section 7

Making 50

Objectives

★ solve mathematical problems
★ explain how the problem was solved
★ use the relationship between addition and subtraction

This is a very open-ended activity which children can tackle at their own level. Children use a number line where only the multiples of 5 are written in to help them find a pair of numbers with the total 50. Because the line is not filled up with numbers, the structure of the number system is clear and can support children in their mental calculation.

You need

• board and marker
• demonstration line with 50 intervals numbered in fives, with pen
• calculator

for each pair:
• desktop line with 50 intervals numbered in fives (*Number line 8*), with pen
• paper and pens/pencils

Working with the children

Write up on the board two or three additions where the answer is 50. Make sure one of these uses numbers where the ones digit is 5.

$$35 + 15 =$$
$$23 + 27 =$$
$$9 + 41 =$$

Ask the children to help you use the demonstration line to work out the answers to these problems. Start with the addition where the ones digit is 5.

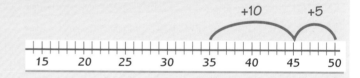

35 jump on 10 is 45, then another 5 makes 50.

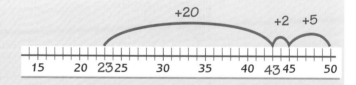

23 jump on 20 is 43, then another 2 makes 45. Then there is still 5 to do ... 50.

Explain that you want all the addition sums to have the answer 50. Now ask a child to suggest a different starting number and help them work out how much they need to add to it to reach 50.

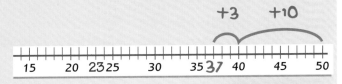

Rosa is starting with 37. An easy jump to do is from 37 to 40. How much is that? ... 3. Rosa, write '+3' above the jump to help you remember.

Now how big is the jump from there to 50? ... So altogether the jump from 37 to 50 is ...?

+3   +10

| | | | | | | | | | | | | | | | | | | | | | | | | | | | | | | | | | | | | |
15   20 23 25   30   35 37 40   45   50

Record the answer on the board.

37 + 13 = 50

Children working independently

Now ask children to invent some other additions where the answer is 50. They should use the desktop lines numbered in fives to help them work out the answers, then write down the corresponding number sentences.

Gathering the children together

Invite various children to read out one of their calculations. (You could quickly vet these to save the children the embarrassment of reading out any that are wrong.)

Invite one of the children to check each calculation on a calculator.

Variations

Simplification

◆ Children could choose starting numbers whose ones digit is 5 or 0.

◆ Ask children to add two numbers to reach a total of 20.

Challenges

◆ Encourage children to do these problems mentally where they can. For harder problems suggest they use an empty number line.

◆ Children can explore ways of reaching 50 from a higher number using subtraction or, with the help of a calculator, they could use multiplication.

◆ Children can explore ways of reaching 10 as imaginatively as they like (for example, $20 - 10$, $99 - 89$, $9\frac{1}{2} + \frac{1}{2}$).

section

7

Spending money

Objectives

★ solve word problems involving money
★ explain how the problem was solved
★ write a number sentence to show how the problem was solved

You need

• OHP and OHT made from *Resource sheet J* (optional)
• demonstration line with 100 intervals numbered in fives, with pen
• board and marker

for each child:
• *Resource sheet J*
• desktop line with 100 intervals numbered in fives (*Number line 7*)(optional)
• paper and pen/pencil

TEACHING POINT

●

You can use number lines to solve number problems – or draw your own partial line.

Children choose items to buy from a stationer's shop. They use a number line or empty line to help them work out how much they spend. With the teacher, they then work out how much change they should have from £1. Number lines where only the multiples of five are written help children see the structure of the number system, and provide a support in their calculations. But children are encouraged to move on to the simpler, do-it-yourself empty number line, which is a big step towards purely mental work.

Working with the children

Show the children the resource sheet, ideally displayed on the OHP. Choose two of the items and ask children how much they estimate the two would cost altogether. Record some of these estimates on the board.

> pencil case and pen
> 35p + 28p
> total will be about
> 60p
> 70p
> 55p

Now demonstrate how to use the line to do the addition involved. Remind children that it is usually a good idea to start with the larger number when adding.

> *So I find 35 on the line. How much do I need to jump on?*

Invite children to suggest methods for adding 28, and choose one or more of these to demonstrate.

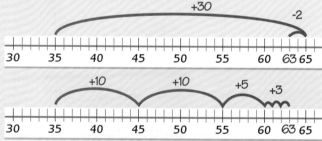

Now demonstrate one or two methods of doing the same calculation with an empty line.

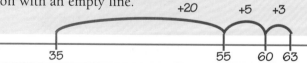

> *I start at 35p. First I add on 20. I need to do 8 more but first I'll do 5 to take me to 60. Then there's ... 3 more. That takes me to 63.*

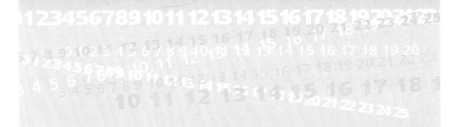

Show how to write the calculation and interpret what it means.

$$35 + 28 = 35 + 20 + 5 + 3 = 63$$

Children working independently

Now give children a copy of the resource sheet and talk through the stages with them. The instructions on the sheet have been left fairly open, so you can choose what individual children should do. To start with, each child should choose two items to buy and complete the calculation. Most children should be able to repeat this several times with different pairs of items. (See 'Variations' for other alternatives.) They can use desktop lines numbered in fives or make their own empty lines.

Gathering the children together

Ask one or two children to demonstrate how they worked out the necessary additions (making sure you choose children who have done it correctly). Then choose one calculation and ask them how they would work out how much money they will have left from £1 (that is, how much change they should expect from a £1 coin). Demonstrate one method, with the children's help, for example:

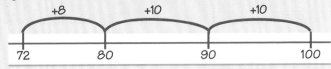

I start at 72, because that is how much Julie spent on her things. Then I start going forwards towards 100p, which is the same as £1. First I do a jump of eight to 80. Then I make jumps of ten towards 100. Say the numbers as I land on them ... 72 and 8 is 80, and 10 is 90, and 10 is 100. That's 28.

Establish with the children how much change there is, and write the calculation on the board.

$$£1 - 72p =$$
$$100p - 72p = 28p$$

Choose another one of the children's calculations and again, with them, work out the change. Use a different method, for example, jumping on 20 instead of two tens.

If appropriate, ask individual children to demonstrate their own calculations for finding the change from £1.

Variations

◆ Provide similar spending problems based on a topic of interest: pet food, gifts, game scores …

◆ Provide problems involving weight, capacity or length. For example: a piece of playground equipment can bear no more than 100 kg of weight; which combinations of children (give their weights) can play on it at the same time? Or: a metre of ribbon is to be made into headbands; which children (give their head circumferences) can have a band from this metre?

Simplifications
◆ Guide children to choose items with the lower prices.

◆ Children can use numbered lines.

Challenges
◆ Children can choose more than two items to buy.

◆ Children can choose more than two items but not spend more than £1.

◆ Children can work out the change from £1 when they do the initial calculation. You could add to the resource sheet, at the end of the instructions to the children: 'I will have …… change from £1.'

section 7

Liquorice shoelace

Objectives

★ solve word problems involving length
★ explain how the problem was solved
★ choose and use appropriate operations

You need

• length of string 76 cm long
• demonstration 0–100 number line, with pen
• board and marker
• prepared word problems

for each table:
• a range of desktop lines with pens
• paper and pens/pencils

Children are asked to find how many 12 cm lengths can be cut from a liquorice shoelace 76 cm long. They are invited to choose a number line method which suits them. This gives you the opportunity to assess children's level of confidence with various number line techniques.

Note that the children only work independently for a short time; this is mainly a class activity.

Working with the children

Show the children the length of string. Ask them to imagine the following scenario. The string is actually made of liquorice. They work in a sweet shop and want to cut this liquorice into strips 12 cm long to sell. How many strips could they get from this 76 cm strip?

Invite ideas as to how to tackle the problem using any kind of number line, numbered or otherwise. Acknowledge all suggestions and choose one or more to talk over with the class, but do not complete the calculation at this stage.

Children of different degrees of confidence may prefer very different methods. For example, one child may suggest using an empty number line while another proposes counting twelve steps at a time along a numbered line.

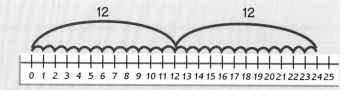

Acknowledge that this would work, but it would be easy to miscount and would take a long time. Encourage methods that use the fact that 12 is made up of 10 and 2, as these are likely to be quicker and easier to check than others.

Children working independently

Ask children to decide for themselves which method to use to find the answer. Give them access to a range of lines and paper. Before they set to work remind them about the details of the problem.

> Liquorice is 76 cm long.
>
> How many 12 cm strips?

Have one or two other problems ready to offer those children who solve this one quickly.

Gathering the children together

Ask one or two children to demonstrate how they worked out the problem (making sure first that they have the answer right).

Pick up on any methods that made use of the fact that 12 is made up of 10 and 2, and help children refine these if necessary.

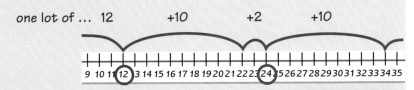

Ring the multiples of 12 on the line (whether numbered, unnumbered or empty) and write these up on the board, reminding children that they can look at the pattern of twelves to check their jumps have landed in the right places.

> jumps of 12
> 12
> 24
> 36
> 48
> 60
> 72

Notice how the ones digits show all the even numbers in turn. That's a way of checking. Suppose after 24 I jumped to 37, would that be right? ... How do you know?

Finally, establish with the children how to interpret the solution.

> *You found that six jumps of 12 got you to 72. How does that help you solve the problem? ... You can get six pieces of liquorice 12 cm long. But the string I showed you was 76 cm, not 72 cm ... There was a little bit left over, 4 cm long.*

Variations

◆ Individual children can invent similar problems and present them to the class to solve.

Simplification

◆ Identify children who choose always to work with numbered lines and support them in using, first, unnumbered lines or lines numbered in fives, and then empty lines.

Challenge

◆ Children can cut their own length of string, measure it and decide how long the sections should be. They then work out how many they can get – and check it by cutting up the string.

section 7

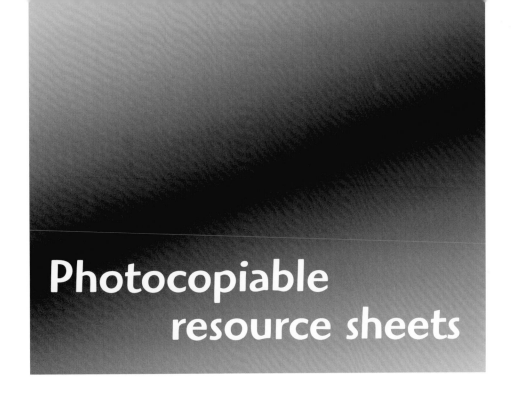

Photocopiable resource sheets

Make your own number line

fill in every number

100   110

fill in every number

105   110

fill in every number

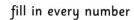

150   155

fill in the tens numbers 110, 120, 130, 140, 150, 160, 170, 180, 190

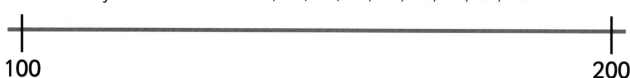

100   200

fill in every number

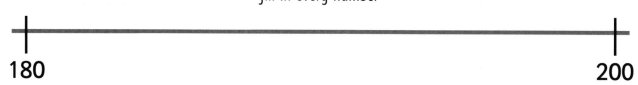

180   200

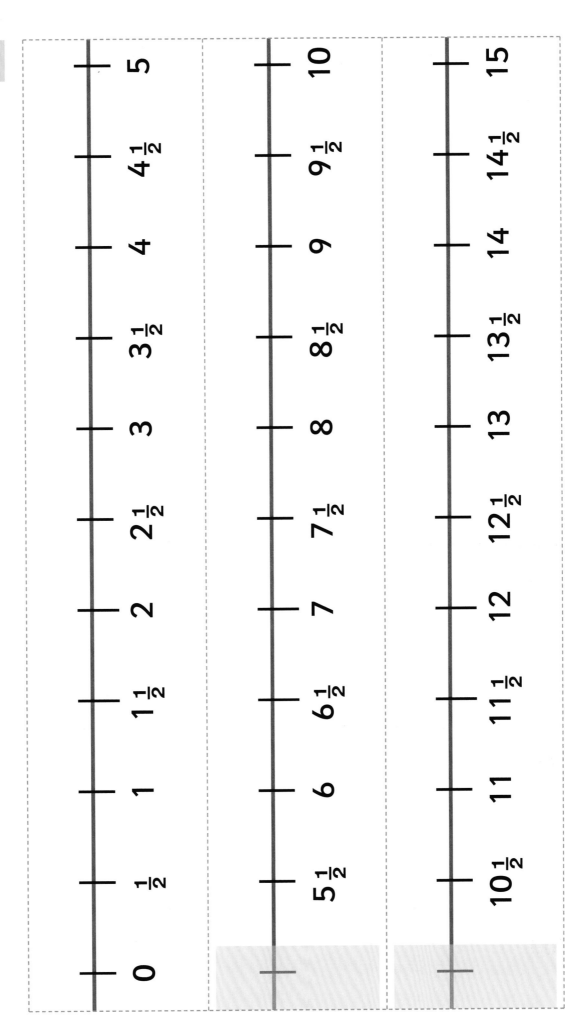

for 'Fit the
fractions in'

$\frac{1}{2}$

1

$1\frac{1}{2}$

2

$2\frac{1}{2}$

3

$3\frac{1}{2}$

4

$4\frac{1}{2}$

5

Resource sheet D

for 'Fit the fractions in'

	$5\frac{1}{2}$	6
$6\frac{1}{2}$	7	$7\frac{1}{2}$
8	$8\frac{1}{2}$	9
$9\frac{1}{2}$	10	

Resource sheet E

for 'Fit the fractions in'

	$10\frac{1}{2}$	11
$11\frac{1}{2}$	12	$12\frac{1}{2}$
13	$13\frac{1}{2}$	14
$14\frac{1}{2}$	15	

Resource sheet F

for 'Fit the fractions in'

	$15\frac{1}{2}$	16
$16\frac{1}{2}$	17	$17\frac{1}{2}$
18	$18\frac{1}{2}$	19
$19\frac{1}{2}$	20	

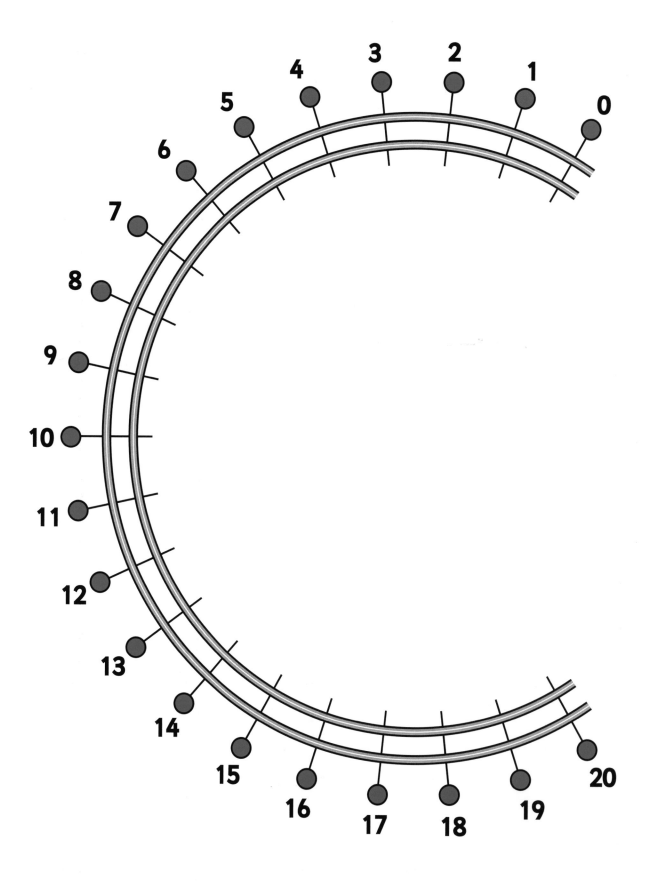

for 'Equal
jumps'

Complete these number lines

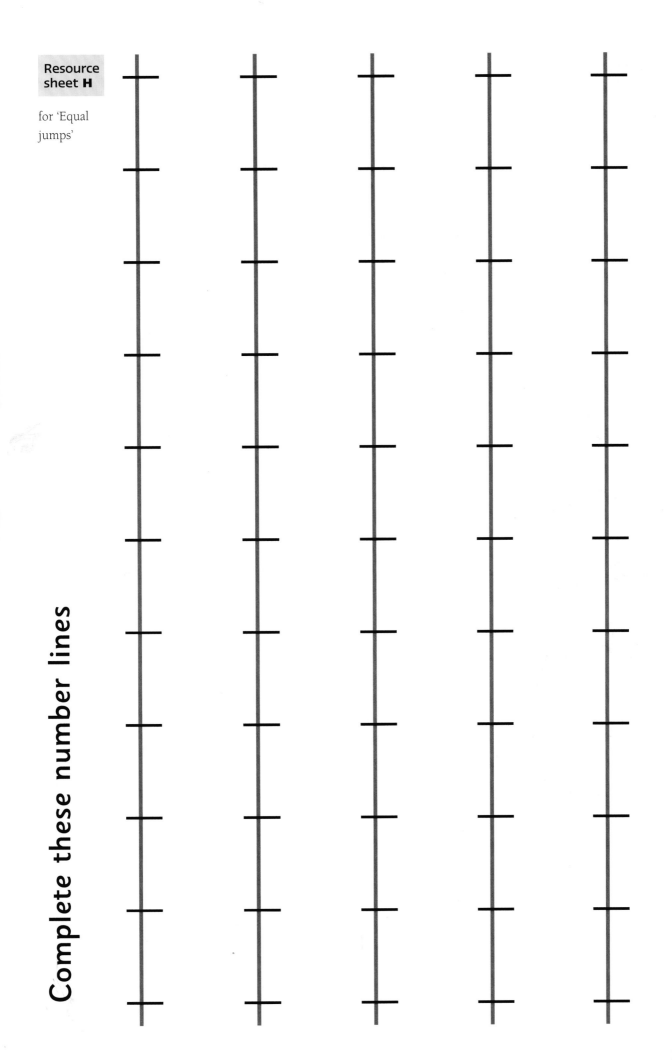

Name ....

The shop is having a sale and taking 15p off each of these items. Work out the new price and write it on the label.

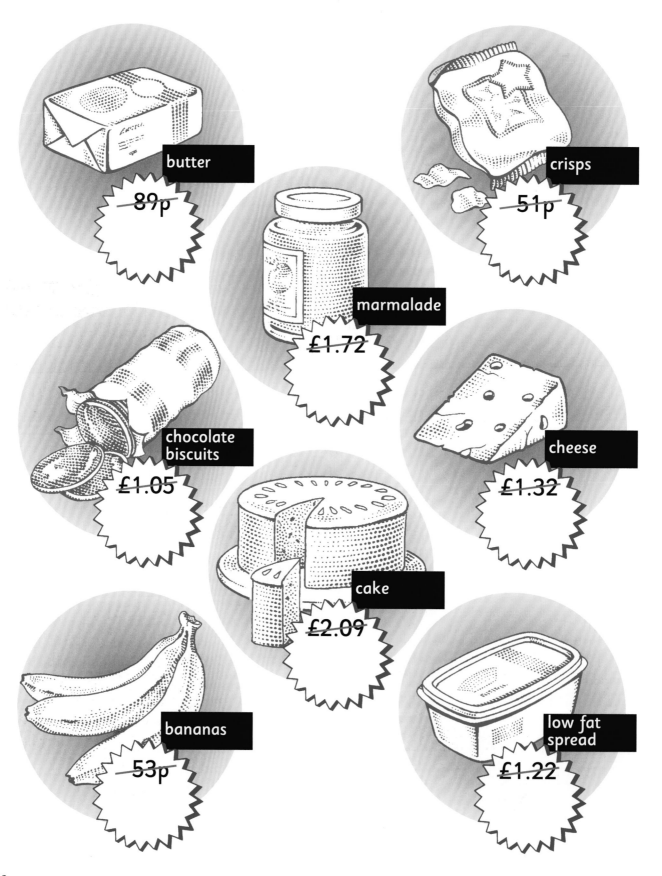

butter

~~89p~~

crisps

~~51p~~

marmalade

~~£1.72~~

chocolate biscuits

~~£1.05~~

cheese

~~£1.32~~

cake

~~£2.09~~

bananas

~~53p~~

low fat spread

~~£1.22~~

What will you buy?

Choose what you want to buy and work out how much it will cost. Copy this and complete it for each calculation you do.

I will buy ....

It will cost ....

This is the number sentence: ....

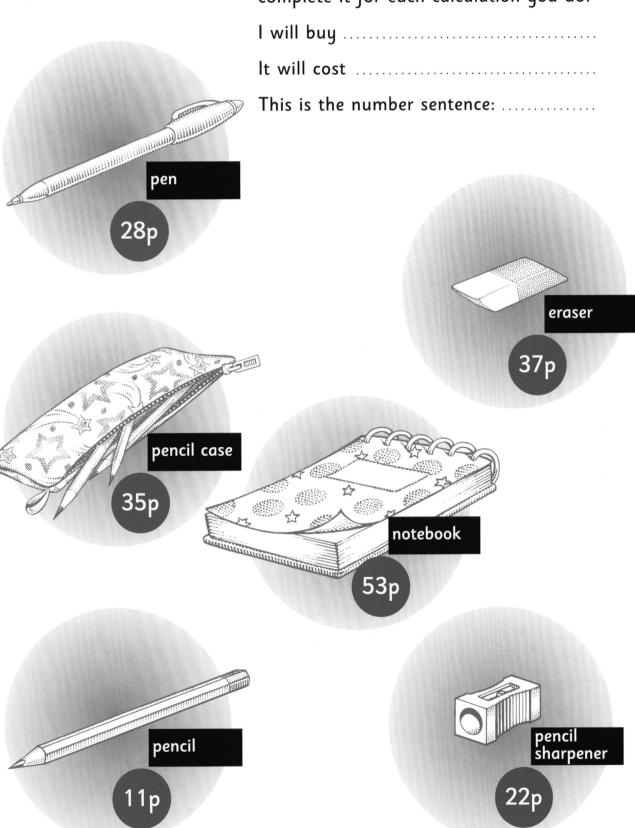

pen
28p

eraser
37p

pencil case
35p

notebook
53p

pencil
11p

pencil sharpener
22p

Photocopiable number lines

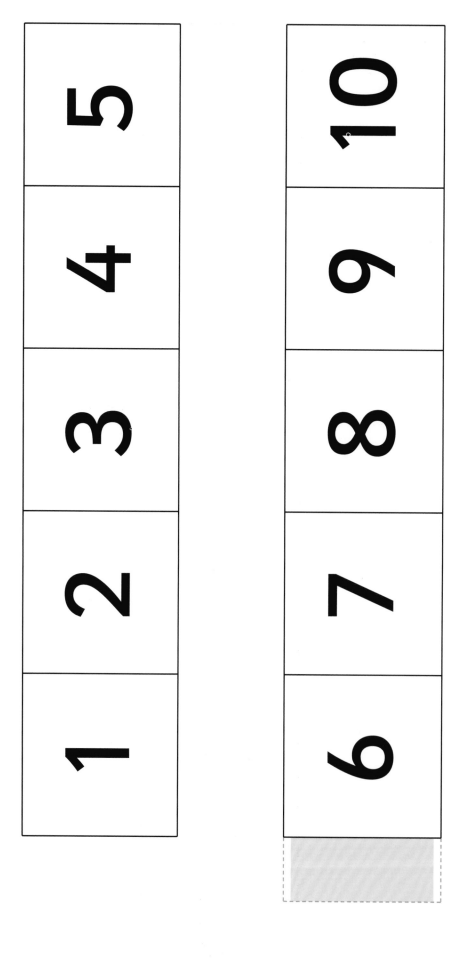

1 2 3 4 5

6 7 8 9 10

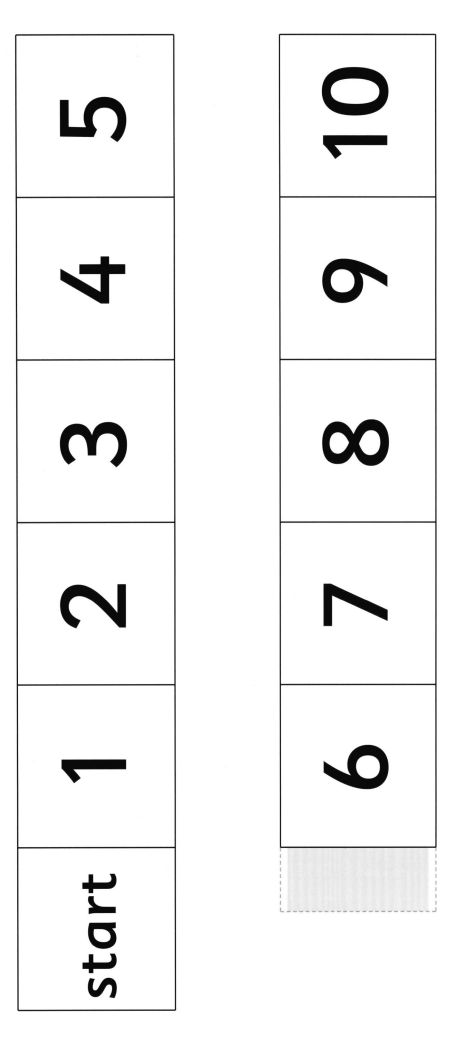

start 1 2 3 4 5

6 7 8 9 10

1	2	3	4	5	6

7	8	9	10	11	12	13

14	15	16	17	18	19	20

Number line 4

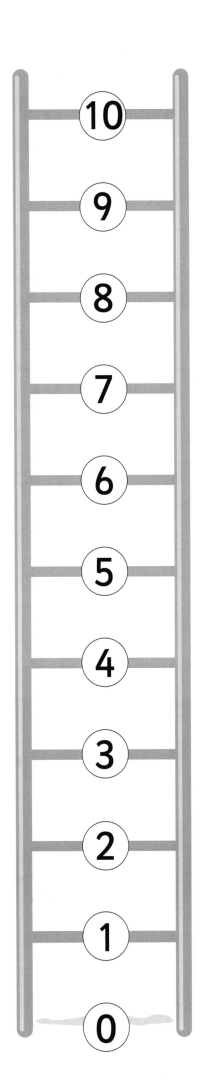

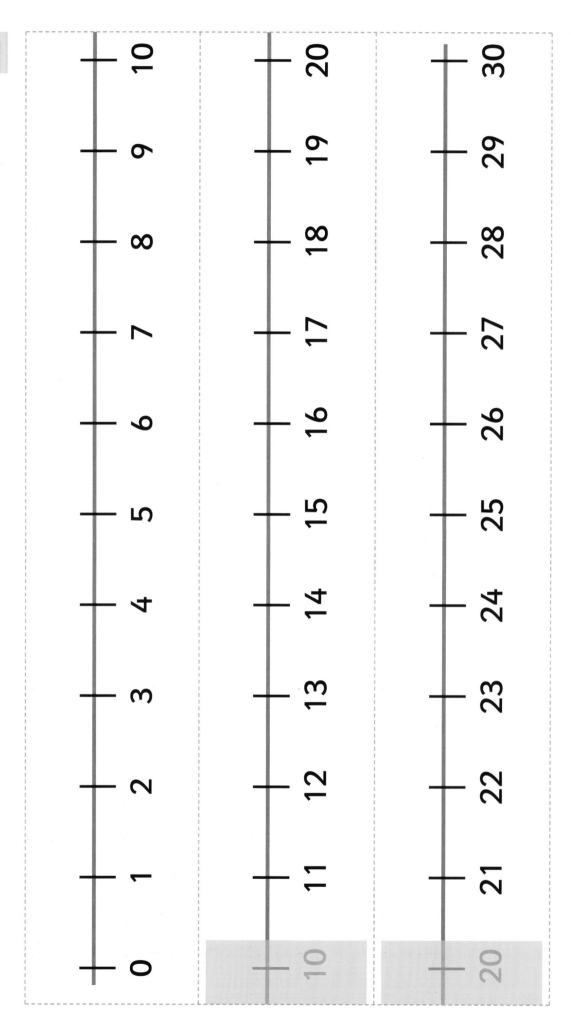

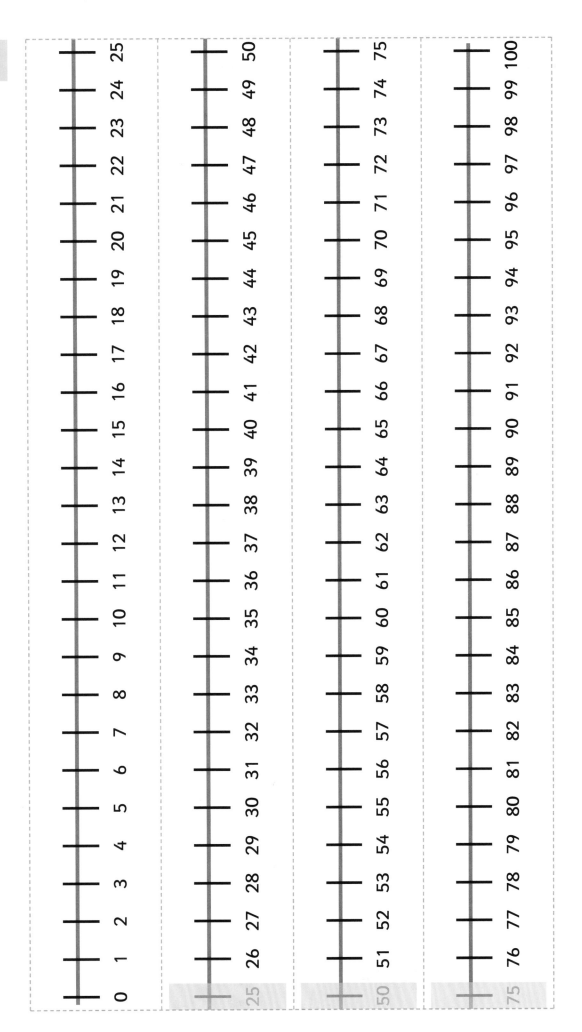

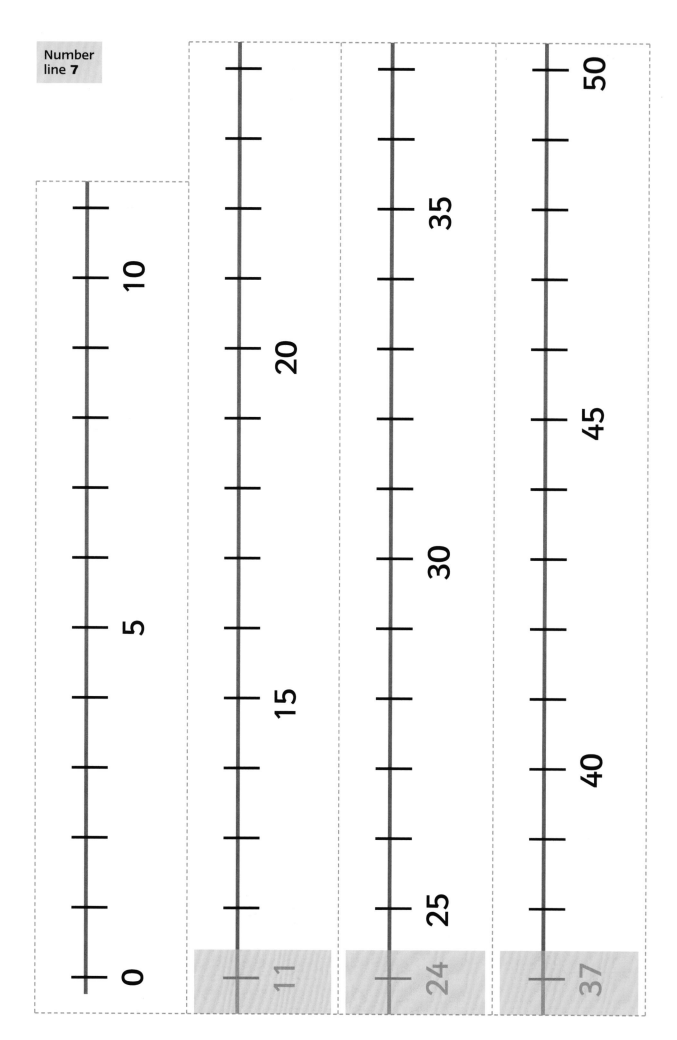

0   5   10

11   15   20

24   25   30   35

37   40   45   50

Number line 7

continued from p122

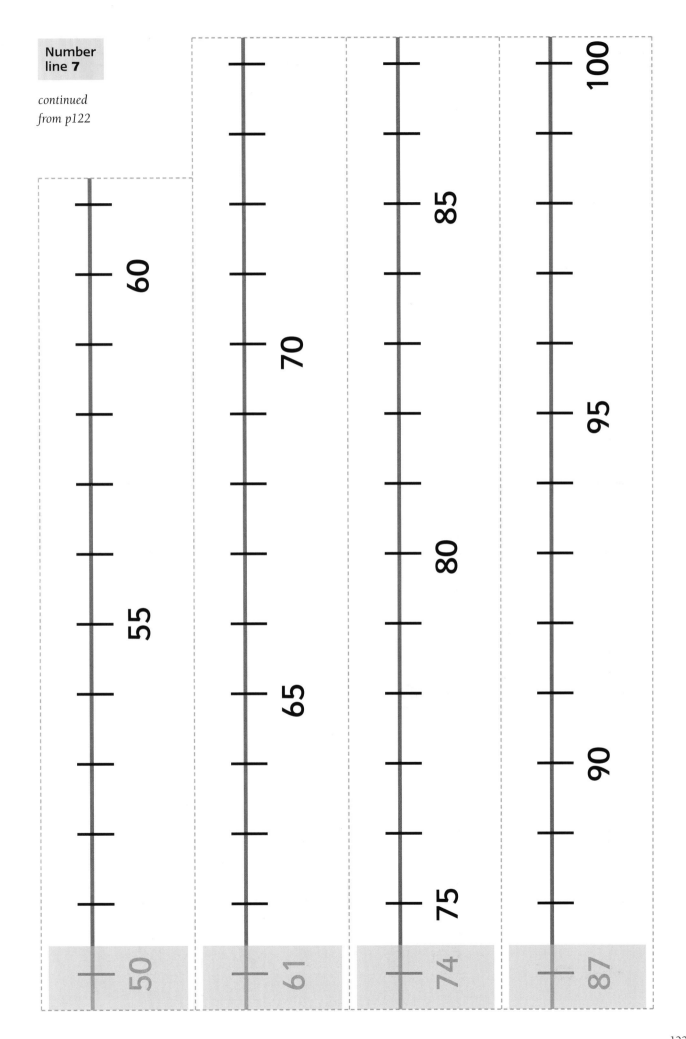

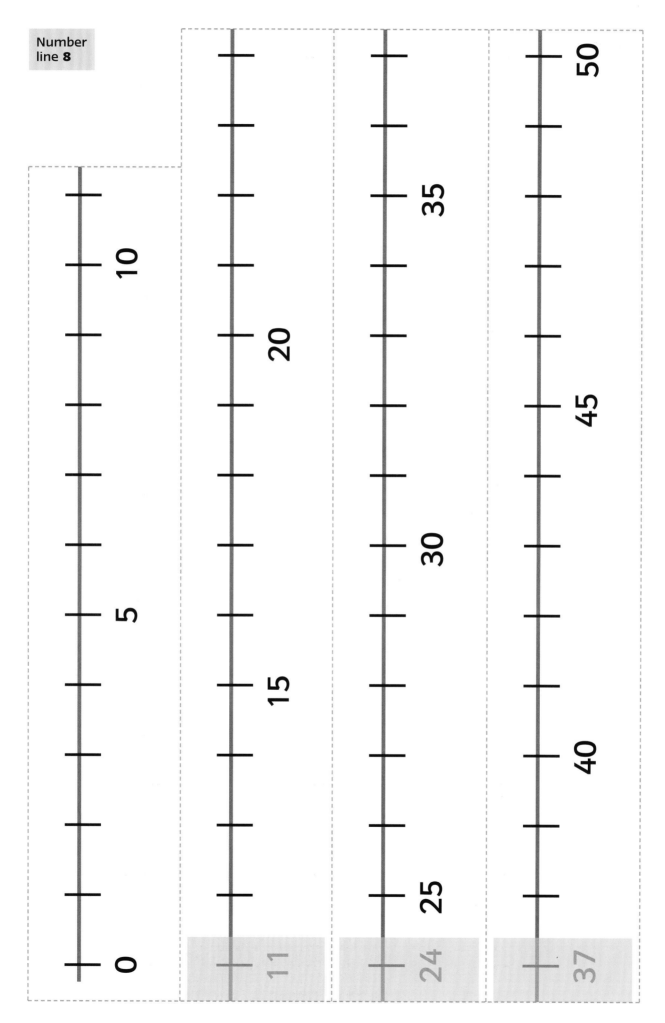

Number line **8**

0   5   10

11   15   20

24   25   30   35

37   40   45   50

124

continued from p126

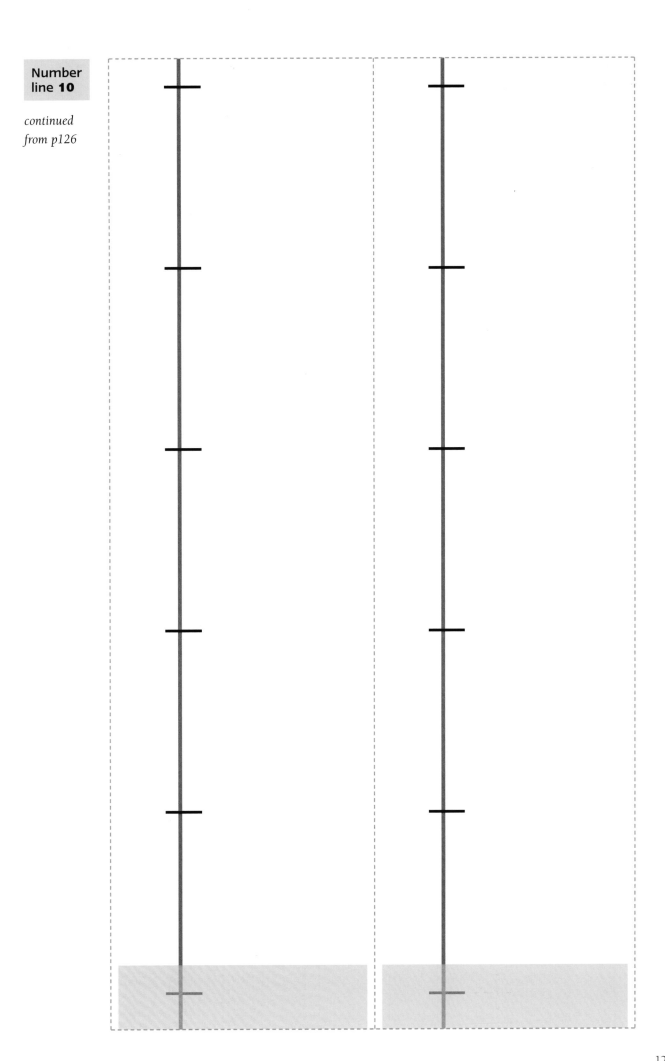

Acknowledgments

- We would like to acknowledge and thank Sue Gifford, whose unpublished work on number lines provided so much of the stimulus – and some of the ideas – for this book, and who read and commented on the draft materials.
- Thanks also to Tamara Bibby who read the book and wrote the introduction.
- And very many thanks to the staff and children at Hargrave Park Primary School, Ridgeway Primary School, Yerbury Primary School and Tufnell Park Primary School, who generously welcomed us into their classrooms to take photographs.
- We are, as ever, indebted to those who trialled the activities in the classroom:

- Justine Abbott and Ennersdale Primary School, London
- Pat Avery and The Magdalen School, Lincolnshire
- Judith Bandtock, Joan Marshall and Bevendean Primary School, Brighton
- Lisa Bloor and The Dale Primary School, Stockport
- Anne Brouart and Hautes Capelles Infant School, Guernsey
- Barbara Carr and Cranford House School, Wallingford
- Muriel Chester and the Southwark BEAM Group
- Peter Clarke, educational consultant
- Shelagh Cosgrow and St Ursula's Infant School, Romford
- Marion Cranmer and Dog Kennel Hill Primary School, London
- Alison Day and Pelham First School, London
- Marie Donagher and St Joseph's RC Primary School, London
- John Ellard and Wellsmead First School, Milton Keynes
- Huw Evans and Herdings Junior School, Sheffield
- Mary Gwilliam and Northfield House Primary School, Leicester
- Ruth Hall and Slinford CE Primary School, West Sussex
- Diane Hargreaves and Langworthy Road County Primary School, Salford
- Clive Harkom and Verney Avenue School, High Wycombe
- JE Harris and Henham and Ugley School, Bishops Stortford
- Pearl Harrison and Dunmow Infants School, Essex
- Senga Harrison, Linda Wileman and St Jude's CE Primary School, London
- Rosemary Harvey and Ashburton Infant School, Croydon
- Sue Hawthorne and Moor Park School, Shropshire
- Carol Heath and West Sussex Special Needs Support Service, West Sussex
- Karen Holman and Long Buckby Junior School, Northamptonshire
- Linda Knock and Oaklands Infants School, Chelmsford
- Karen Jones and Priory Lower School, Bedford
- Sandra Lemming and Bradfields Secondary Special School, Kent
- Janis Lockett and Kingsway Independent School, Wigan
- Caroline Logan and Whitgreave Primary School, Staffordshire
- Chris Lumb and Tyersal First School, Bradford
- Joy Lynch and St George's Cathedral School, London
- Adele Markey and Bury and Whitefield Junior Primary School, Bury
- Anne Marsh and Gillingham Wyke Primary School, Dorset
- Linda Marshall and Quarry View Infant School, Sunderland
- Vivienne Millward and Low Bentham County Primary, Lancaster
- Margaret Misson and Monks Orchard Primary School, Croydon
- Mandy Morgan and Malpas Church Infant School, Newport
- Caroline Nias and Wadhurst Primary School, East Sussex
- Carol Palmer and Valley Road Infant School, Sunderland
- Angela Perry, Okehampton Primary School, Devon
- Jane Prothero and Grimes Dyke School, Leeds
- Susan Robinson and Webber's CE School, Wellington
- Pauline Sear and Spooner Row CP School, Norfolk
- Ana Smallwood and Highgate Primary School, London
- Christine Smith and Orchard Way Primary School, Croydon
- Lis Stuart and Grange Infant School, Northampton
- Carolyn Wallis and St Nicholas House Junior School, Hemel Hempstead
- Aimee Warren and Bishop Winnington Ingram CE School, Ruislip
- Sian Watson and Dunmow Infants School, Essex
- Gay Whent and Wood Ley County Primary School, Stowmarket